CW01645109

Patricia Pegg

December 1996

A VERY PRIVATE HERITAGE

A VERY PRIVATE HERITAGE

THE FAMILY PAPERS OF SAMUEL THEODORE MANDER

1853 – 1900

PATRICIA PEGG

First published by Images Publishing (Malvern Ltd) Great Britain 1996,
The Wells House, Holywell Road, Malvern Wells,
Worcestershire WR14 4LH

British Library Cataloguing in Publication Data

A catalogue record for this book is available from the British Library

ISBN 1 897817 85 1

Designed and produced by Images.
Printed and Bound in Great Britain by Bookcraft, Bath, Avon.

Theodore Mander and his family at Wightwick Manor in the mid 1890's.

ACKNOWLEDGEMENTS

All the archive papers and photographs held at Wightwick Manor belong to Anthea Mander Lahr; from the start she has been unstinting in her enthusiasm and support. Without her permission to delve into the archives and to use the family photographs this book would not exist.

Following the death of Lady Mander in 1988, the archivist Mark Weaver spent some nine months at Wightwick sorting out the family papers. Letters, documents and photographs covering a period of more than a 100 years were scattered all over the house and it was his valuable preliminary work which provided the basis for all my future research.

I am very grateful to Monisha Garnham (Alan Mander's daughter) and Peter Nevile (Marjorie Mander's son) for their generosity in answering all my questions about their parents.

Julian Gibbs is the Historic Buildings representative of the National Trust in the Mercia region. I would like to thank him for his support. He is known for his enthusiastic response to exciting new projects and I am so pleased that was how he viewed the production of a book on Theodore Mander.

The photograph were all copied for the printers by the photographer Cliff Guttridge, of Uppington in Shropshire. Some of the originals were rather faded and difficult to see. "They won't be when I've finished with them" he said. As you can see, he was right.

Geoffrey Hancock, former Second Master at Tettenhall College, has put up with my questions very patiently. I would like to thank him for permission to quote from his books.

A letter was sent to Wightwick from Malcolm Shifin of The Victorian Turkish Bath Data Base; it contained information we had not seen before and I am pleased to be able to use it in the endnotes.

Producing this book has involved a number of people with expertise in all sorts of areas; they have all been asked at odd times for diverse pieces of information and everyone has taken the time and trouble to respond. I am indebted to all of them; – David Bennett, Fred Clegg, Beverley and Edward Craft, Stan Hill of The Black Country Society, Edith Husk, John Kynnersley, David, Matthew and Jonathan Pegg, Stephen Ponder; Jenny Hancock, Antony Slack and J. Woodward of Ashford, Kent.

My first contact with Tony Harold of Images was over the telephone when I made a tentative call to see if anyone might be interested in my book. He was, and I am very grateful for his encouragement. Since then the staff at Images has worked very hard on my behalf. I want to thank them all, especially Catherine Whiting for her patience and support.

Finally, the National Trust Property Manager at Wightwick, Monty Smith, was the first person to listen to my ideas about a book based on the personal papers of Theodore Mander. He has put up with me working in odd places all over Wightwick, allowed me to use the photocopier at inconvenient times, tactfully given good advice, provided useful bits of information and when things were getting rather bogged down, had the bright idea of producing a public performance based on the archive papers – organising it clarified everything and gave me the impetus to continue. I am very grateful to him for all his help and interest.

INTRODUCTION

Wightwick, recorded in the Doomsday Book as "Wistwic" lies to the west of Wolverhampton at the point where the suburbs merge into the fields of Shropshire. It still retains something of its previous rural character even though it is situated on the edge of a solidly built up area reaching back into the centre of the town. After the First World War a limited amount of house building began on land sold by the owners of the few large estates in the area. As the century progressed, more and more building was carried out on plots which became smaller and smaller. By the 1960's and 1970's the suburban Avenues and Drives were well established, and now most of the land is divided into small individual plots. Wightwick stands on a high sandstone ridge running along the western borders of Wolverhampton and many of the roads cut into the rock are steep, narrow and restrictive: a number of the old boundary lanes and roads still remain. This and the fact that some ancient trees still flourish, has helped to retain a certain individual character within the suburban landscape.

Dotted among the twentieth century houses in Wightwick are a few older properties. One of them, Wightwick House, was built in the eighteenth century and a hundred years later in the 1880's it was owned by a Mr Harper, known by the Mander family as Uncle Harper. He had married Janetta Mander in 1844 and shortly after this joined the family firm of Mander Brothers.

I

The Mander paint and varnish firm was founded in Wolverhampton in 1773 by Benjamin Mander, whose father had moved to Wolverhampton from Warwickshire in the middle of the 18th century. In 1845, under Benjamin's grandsons, the brothers Charles and Samuel, the firm became Mander Brothers. It was 1853 when Samuel Mander's first surviving child was born; christened Samuel Theodore he was always known as Theodore. This became something of a tradition for Samuel and Mary Mander; their two younger sons, Benjamin Howard and Bertram Martin, were always known as Howard and Martin, and although in later years Mary rejected her pet name of Polly, Jemima, Ellen and Charlotte were always known as Mima, Nellie and Lotte.

It was after the birth of Theodore that Samuel Mander began to keep a notebook in which he recorded the progress of his son and subsequently that of his sisters. The birth of Benjamin Howard is noted just before the last entry in the book, in 1861. Seven and a half years later in 1869, Bertram Martin was born, too late for inclusion in his father's records.

The Mander family, photographed in the 1870's.
Left to right standing . . . Howard, Samuel S. Mander, Nellie.
Left to right seated . . . Mima, Lotte, Mary Mander, Theodore, Mary.
In front . . . Martin.

Starting with Samuel's notebook, all of Theodore Mander's life is documented in surprising detail through his own letters and, following his father's example, through the notebooks he kept; Samuel's letters to him when he was small and then away at school bridge some of the early gaps. Letters from the family and friends were saved as well.

One of his father's early instructions was for Theodore to be "anything but being lazy." From the evidence in the archive papers he took this order very seriously. For the first time, when he was seven, Theodore kept a record of a holiday spent in Hastings and this started a practice which continued through most of his life. Later he kept notebooks on visits to factories with accounts of manufacturing processes, reports on sermons attended, scientific observations on plants, birds and animals and, at the same time, he wrote long, interesting letters occasionally indulging in poetic descriptions of places he visited.

After his entry into the family firm and his marriage, Theodore never again had time for such detailed letters and diaries but he did, to a lesser extent, follow his father's practice of keeping notes on the development of his children;

during the last years of his life an interest in gardening resulted in yet another notebook with comments on the weather, the prevalence of mildew and greenfly and rooks!

In 1881 he was elected to the Council for the first time, and went on to serve on a number of committees. At the time of his death he was chairman of the School Board, governor of the local grammar school and of his old school, Tettenhall College. He was a borough and county magistrate, a governor of Birmingham University, and a member of the Royal Commission for the British section of the Paris Exhibition – "anything but being lazy"!

There are few people whose last illness and death are reported in detail, but Theodore Mander died in office while Mayor of Wolverhampton and the story of his life is rounded off by accounts in the local newspapers of his final illness, death and civic funeral in September 1900.

II

Letters and diaries are bound to reveal something of the character of the writer but those relating to Theodore Mander, covering a lifetime of more than forty years, chart his development too, from infancy to maturity. There are letters in the archives concerning Theodore, from other members of the family, and newspaper cuttings of tributes paid to him at the time of his death. When all these papers are put together, an intimate portrait is revealed which appears to be so consistent that through forty years the same observations about his character are repeated several times. When he was eight, his father wrote "he is naturally very shy and unfriendly to strangers and backward in accosting them," and a teacher reported the eleven year old Theodore as being " . . . so very shy and undemonstrative with strangers, that very little of his real character and capabilities can be known for some time." That this remained so, to some extent throughout his life, can be gathered from one of the obituaries printed in a local paper in 1900. "There was about the Mayor a certain reserve . . . which did not attract all people as they are attracted to some popular men . . ." It is obvious that initially he was difficult to know and this worried his father, whose letters suggest that, unlike his son, he was a more ebullient, lively man.

III

Theodore Mander was a true Victorian. He was born in 1853 when Victoria had been on the throne for sixteen years and he died four months before the end of her reign. For most of his forty seven years his strong religious faith dominated every aspect of his life; in this he was influenced by the early guidance of his parents but he was also typical of his age. In a period remarkable for the speed of economic and social change, serious discussion of theological questions, with a constant emphasis on personal morality and self-discipline, was a lasting subject of interest. It was this serious attitude towards religion which characterised the nineteenth century Englishman and provided such a shocking contrast when he travelled abroad. Theodore encountered what he described as a "large class of student infidels" while he was studying in Germany and was shocked by their apparent ignorance of the Bible. While the strength of Sunday observance in England was in marked contrast to that on the Continent, it was religious observance that divided rather than united the English at this time.

After the French Revolution, in England a period of economic uncertainty was exacerbated by the Napoleonic Wars and the aftermath of the war with America. Prices rose and unemployment grew. Against this background, grievances over the privileges of the Established Church resulted in fierce attacks in the Radical Press, with rioting mobs and Dissenters uniting in opposition to the High Tory party and the Church of England. Nonconformist preachers, whose work was often concentrated on the disenfranchised urban poor (a mass of people largely ignored by the Church) were seen as imparting Radical doctrines, and so a great many laws which discriminated against all Nonconformists were introduced.

From the eighteenth century the Manders had been Nonconformists and as such, suffered under many existing laws: for example, Lord Hardwicke's Marriage Act of 1753 laid down that all marriages must be conducted by clergy of the Established Church, while entrance to Oxford or Cambridge Universities was open only to Church of England communicants.

In the 1820's with the widespread demands for reforms growing on all sides, slow changes began to be made. With the First Reform Bill of 1832 limited voting rights were granted to the disenfranchised, followed by a number of Acts of Parliament that changed some of the circumstances contributing to the unpopularity of the Church. Discrimination against Nonconformists took a little longer to change, but with the Marriage Act of 1836, the Act of 1753 was rescinded and, as long as the newly established Registrars of Births, Marriages and Deaths were notified, marriages were allowed in chapels and in Roman Catholic and Nonconformist churches.

When Theodore was born in 1853, a large proportion of primary schools, particularly those in rural areas, were run by the Church of England. The British and Foreign School Society helped to set up a number of Nonconformist schools and Roman Catholic schools were often established through the efforts of local individuals.

In 1863, a group of Congregationalists and Baptists in Wolverhampton bought a house in the suburbs for £3,700 and set up a school for the children of Free Churchmen. It was called the Tettenhall Proprietary School and began with 15 boys. Samuel Mander was one of the proprietors; he bought shares worth £750, and from 1864 until 1871 Theodore was a pupil at the school.

When Theodore was 16 and studying for a year in France, his father sent him a letter full of observations on the passage through Parliament of the 1870

Education Bill during which lively debates took place between "the sides into which English life is divided on almost all questions, the stand-stills and the progressives . . . a grand struggle is expected." This was the bill that eventually guaranteed non-sectarian primary education for all children.

Educational opportunities for students were widening too. London University was established in 1827 with the aim of promoting undenominational education. Unlike Oxford and Cambridge, there were no theological entrance tests for staff or students and the traditional emphasis placed on Classical studies was replaced by a tendency towards modern subjects, such as science. All this meant that when Theodore was 19 in 1872, London University was so well established that his father's cousin in recommending it as a place at which to matriculate, stated "The examination is not generally looked upon as a simple one. I believe it is admitted to be more trying than the preliminary ones at Oxford and Cambridge."

IV

Whatever the reforms passed by Parliament, a great many people still found the notion of Nonconformism dreary; it is true that the serious nature of some evangelicals led to a stark existence eschewing any indulgence in the pleasures of life. Seen from the outside, teetotal families like the Manders, who did not dance and who, like Theodore, spent time distributing religious tracts and lay preaching, do sound dull. That is where the evidence contained in personal letters and diaries can confute the stereotypes. The proselytising nature of Samuel Mander, jumping out of his letters with such vividness, was tempered by common sense and a loving nature. He does display in his notebook the typical concern manifested so often by devout Victorians for the moral development of their children. When Theodore was 3½ his father observed "the signs of a fallen human nature have been but too apparent in him." This stern assessment referred to "selfishness, petulance, waywardness." His parents chose to correct his bad behaviour gently and with some subtlety, always stressing that the approval of God was to be gained by good behaviour.

"Today Theodore having had some sugar plums given him asked for more and was denied. Still soliciting and tears being near his eyes, his Mama said "Well Theodore, you may take some more if you please, but I would rather you did not." He immediately laid them aside without a word – remained silent a little, as if reflecting and then said "Mama, I have pulled up another weed have I not?" This was an allusion to the idea that the heart is a garden in which grow noxious weeds which it is our business to pull up by acts of self denial."

From the beginning he was encouraged by his father to take a delight in the natural world, and he wrote to the 5 year old Theodore "I should like you to be a little Botanist and know all about the plants and trees that God has made to grow all around us." Exercise was encouraged. "Do you walk out much and on the shore? I want you to walk a great deal and run and jump and climb etc . . ."

Later, in Theodore's papers there are references to art galleries visited, to books read, and a common place book begun when Theodore was nineteen is entitled "Choice Extracts of Various Authors." Even though his studies were concerned later with the modern subject of science, he had a good grounding in classics too, and all this, together with his interest in architecture, was fostered by his father. There must have been many men like Samuel Mander, who did not conform to the unsubtle image of the typical nineteenth century hard headed business man, obsessed with commerce and blind to the finer things of life.

When Theodore was born, eighty years had passed since the establishment of the Mander firm, and there had been time to relax into prosperity. However, the strong Nonconformist tendency running through Samuel Mander's branch of the family gave rise to a pronounced social conscience combined with practical humanitarianism[1]. It was inevitable that they with many other Nonconformists, aligned themselves with the Liberal party, always seeing new opportunities for reform and setting themselves against those Samuel Mander had described as the "stand-stills" or Tories. In 1895 Theodore was invited to stand as the Parliamentary Liberal candidate for Mid-Worcester. Although he declined, in 1929, his eldest son Geoffrey entered Parliament as the Liberal member for East Wolverhampton.

V

In 1887 Theodore Mander bought the Wightwick estate, which included an ancient house and about a hundred acres of land. It was a convenient site, next door to Uncle Harper's house and although in a rural setting only a carriage drive away from the Mander Brothers' factory in the centre of Wolverhampton.

The new house built there by Theodore in 1887 and extended in 1893 was decorated in the fashionable style of the day, with products from the William Morris firm, together with oriental carpets and porcelain. Wightwick Manor was inherited by Geoffrey Mander on the death of his parents and in 1937 he and his wife gave the house to the National Trust.

In recent years due to the growth of interest in the work of William Morris and the Arts and Crafts movement, Wightwick has received much attention from art historians, journalists and the public. To many people, the name of Theodore Mander is irrevocably linked now with that of William Morris but there is no evidence that they ever met.

Theodore Mander died nearly a hundred years ago. In public, he was a quiet, shy man but now, with the discovery of so many personal papers, we are able to know him more intimately than many of the people who actually met him.

A VERY PRIVATE HERITAGE

1853

Extracts from Samuel Mander's notebook, in which he recorded his children's early years. The first notes, written retrospectively, were begun in October 1855.

Notice respecting our dear children whom may God bless and save! To be inscribed on each successive birthday while they are spared to us and we to them.

June 1851

This day, our first little one (a boy, still born) was brought into a world it was not to gaze upon. It first opened its eyes (as we believe) in the abodes of the blest. Though about six weeks before its time, it was really a very nice child and very pleasing to look upon. Its little coffin was laid on that of its dear grandmama Mander.

February 25th, 1853

This day we had the pleasure of embracing our first living child, a boy, to whom we gave the name of Samuel Theodore – meaning we had asked him of the Lord and now desired to give him up to Him.

Theodore (for so we call him) was a very good baby; no trouble at all at night. Always has enjoyed good health, though by no means stoutly built. Cut his teeth early and easily. Was vaccinated at 4 months with success. Walked alone at 13½ months. Talked early and very distinctly. At 2 years of age began to talk very hesitatingly and loosely which we took care to check.

When about two and a quarter years old, we remarked with some degree of concern that he manifested great timidity at being left alone. He frequently showed signs of fear at the dark, at unusual noises, or shadows on the wall, at a dog etc. As soon as he could repeat words he was taught the little verse "Gentle Jesus" etc. which for a short time constituted his morning and evening prayer. A little later he was taught to add "Pray God bless Papa and Mama, Aunt and Uncle and Jane and Margaret" and he would often mention others besides.

Theodore never requires sleep during the day, nor has done since about 2 years old, but being dressed between 7.30 to 8, continues active and wakeful all day till about 7 when he is put to bed and then is usually got to sleep with difficulty.

Hitherto we have not thought it desirable to take him to Chapel regularly. Very occasionally he goes, just as a treat, and then he generally behaves very well, but manifests no wish to go, preferring to stay at home and play.

Chester April 23rd, 1853
My Dearest Wife,
Though I do intend to post this this evening because tomorrow is the Lord's day, I must just write you a few lines with little news etc. I had an interesting conversation with a Roman Catholic Priest in (the) Rail Carriage as I came. He got in with me at WH. I handed to him one of those "Letters to Dr. Raffles" and he very soon handed it back to me with a contemptuous smile playing about his mouth. I asked him his objections; he stated them and I endeavoured to answer them as well as I could. I told him I conceived (the) doctrine of a personal coming of Christ was plainly taught in Scripture and also that He will reign on earth for 1,000 years. He said that as to the former, everyone believed it, but (the) latter was (the) product of my own imagination and had nothing in Scripture to sustain it. I pointed him to the 1st. Acts and XIV of Zechariah. These he said, had nothing to prove my assertions. But when I read to him Revelations XX 1-6 he seemed surprised as though it was quite new to him; he took the book out of my hand and appeared to read the whole chapter through, both of us very silent. When he had done he gave me the book back with a "Y.e.s"! I just read to him in corroboration part of Isaiah XI and David II 44 and VII 13 and 14. He remained mute and nothing more was said on the question, the weather was referred to and we ceased to converse. I did pray that this little circumstance might be blessed to him and I hope it will. There certainly was a remarkable change from confident and contemptuous demeanour to a silence which seemed to imply conviction.

I reached Chester in safety, for which I thank the Lord. I found sister and Mr Harper, the former well and the latter poorly, his stomach or bowels out of order, in fact, suffering from his old complaint.

Sunday 4.30 pm
We have just had John Weaver here. I was talking to him about baby, how he is fed and so forth. He gave it as his decided opinion that no farinacerus (sic) food ought to be given to a child till it is some 6 months old. It should have, in default of its mother's milk, cow's milk diluted with water, or what is better, cream and water; of course in the latter case using much more water than in the former . . .

I have been thinking about you and our dear little one a good deal. I expect you would have a disturbed night though I suppose Jane would sleep with you. Bless him. I trust he is the Lord's. May He in His great mercy shield him (from) all evil influences from man or devil. May He fill him with Himself! I hope and trust you have had a good day today, much more of the Lord's presence with you. That and that alone makes heaven. O to have more of it, more of Him . . .

The Lord bless you my dearest and lift up the light of His countenance upon you and give you peace . . .

Dear sister cannot return with me nor come over for some time to come; she thanks you for your invite.

Now dear, faith! hope! love! these three. The Lord make us to abound in them more and more!

Bless you, farewell, Your affectionate husband, Samuel.

A bunch of kisses for little Master Theodore.

Samuel Small Mander

Great Malvern[2] September 19th, 1853
My dear Wife,
Your little note was duly received on Saturday. Glad to hear you are going on so comfortably and baby too.

Yesterday I enjoyed much. In the morning walked about 1½ miles to hear a Mr Turner a man of no sect, but yet not a Plymouth Brother. He preached from Heb: XI (2/8) By faith Abram being called of God to go etc. etc. Walked there and back with Mr Baillie, the son of a Scottish Laird and of high connections who is also one of the patients. He is very pious and intelligent. On Friday Dr. G. had a party, a lady of rank and of consequence a relation of Mr Baillie's, and Mr Hodkins or some such name, an East Indian Judge and some others. Mr Turner was present and we had singing and prayers and very interesting conversation afterwards. I had no idea that Dr. Grindrod was so valuable a man. He is the author of the great prize essay entitled "Bacchus" and travelled the country, I am informed, for about 6 years lecturing on the teetotal question at his own expense. He has spent I hear about £10,000 on promoting that cause. He is a most liberal Philanthropist, enlightened, agreeable and truly Christian man. His religion shines forth continually. He has a sweet spirit and his society renders this place very attractive. Last evening I went to Church with Cousin. She is poorly today, having had a spasmodic attack. I feel better. Before breakfast this morn, walked to St Ann's Well and drank of the Waters. Since breakfast had a 5 mile walk, came home in good perspiration and tired and then had a sheet dripping with cold water thrown all over me . . .

Samuel Mander's notebook. Theodore was 3 years 7 months.

September 27th, 1856
During the year which has passed since our last memorandum respecting our dear boy, Samuel Theodore, the signs of a fallen human nature have been but too apparent in him. His prevailing disposition is by no means good. Selfishness, petulance, waywardness have unmistakenly appeared. They have not been increased, we hope we can say with truth, by mismanagement. On the contrary we and his nurse too, have endeavoured by forbearance and kindness mingled with firmness and occasional severity to check their growth. We have prayed for him and used what means we could and not seldom have we been cheered by witnessing indications of a kindlier and more genial nature . . .

Addressed to Sea View House, Crescent Road, Rhyl.

Wolverhampton September 21st, 1856
My dear boy,

This morning I was much grieved to part from you as I did. I wanted you to kneel down with your Papa and Mama that we might ask the great God, our Heavenly Father to take care of us and bless us while I was away from you and you know you would not kneel down with us. This made one feel very sorry because I know that if you do not love to pray to God you cannot be good and happy. Now I love you very much and I think you love your Papa too: do then try to be a good boy and that will make me very glad and Mama will be very glad too and we shall all be very happy, Baby and Jane too and if you are good

God will love you and teach you to love Him. So now I send you a kiss, I (could not) let you come to the station to see me off. Now remember, I shall ask Mama how you behave and I hope to hear that you do every thing that she and Jane tells you, so now Mama will kiss you from me, your loving father.

My dearest, I felt it might do well if I sent Theodore a line or two Please read it to him simply as it is and it may be poor. I hope God will bless it.

Addressed to Master Mander, Water Street. Rhyl.

Penn Fields, Wolverhampton September 25th, 1857
My dear boy,

I have written 3 or 4 letters to your dear Mama since I left you all and now I really think it is your turn to have one. It seems a long time since I left you and I can tell you, I want to see you again very much indeed. I want to tell you what the Great God has told me about you. Shall I tell you what it is? Yes! I fancy I hear you say "I should like to know." Well then it is this. God has told me that you are His little boy and He has given you to your dear Mama and me that we may take care of you for a time all the while you are a boy and till He is ready to send for you and we are to do all we can to get you ready to go when He does send for you. We are to tell you about Him; about the beautiful place where he lives, that is Heaven you know; about the happy people who live there with Him and what we are to do to get there. O that I could say that everybody went to live with our Father in Heaven! Many, O how many will never see it. Those are the wicked who will not love God and do as He wishes then and you know what becomes of them.

But now my dear boy you are by the sea – the wonderful sea. Stand there and look across it as far as you can, as far as where it meets the sky and then say "My Father made you great sea and He tells you how far you may come up and when your tide must go back again and you cannot come the breadth of my little finger further than He bids you. Great as you are He can hold you in the hollow of His hand . . . This world is my Father's great nursery but Heaven is my house." Will you say so? . . .

Samuel Mander's notebook

December 28th, 1857
Today we have had a little juvenile party to commemorate for the third time the birthday (which was on Sunday 27th.) of our dear little Mary Jane, whom we usually call "Polly." . . .

I record with pleasure and I hope some measure of gratitude, that the general progress made by our dear little Polly during the 2 past years has been satisfactory. The most remarkable feature of her character or conduct has been and still is her imitation of her Brother Theodore in everything. She says what he says and does what he does. This is a circumstance of great importance, in as much as if *he* be well trained and well conducted, she will be his faithful follower and disciple. And we have observed with much pleasure a marked improvement in him of late, so that his influence on her is now generally good . . .

January 9th, 1858
From the date of our last notice of Theodore, up to a recent period we remarked with anxiety much petulance, waywardness and disobedience which seemed to increase. He would scarcely ever speak to anyone who came to the house or whom he met by the way and our friends seemed to fear we should have much trouble with him. We were convinced at last that a change of nurse was indispensable and so after much consideration and prayer, Jane Neweus who had nursed them carefully and faithfully from their birth was made housemaid and Eleanor Barnet took her place. The result has, so far, shown the wisdom of change. There is now a very marked improvement in Theodore in all respects. He is more obedient and amiable, his manners are much improved and his mind, being more fully occupied, gives tokens of intelligence which make him very interesting.

An incident or two is recorded to show the kind of influence brought to bear upon him and its present effects. Eleanor had made a rule that if she had occasion to speak to them twice, they were to go in the corner for a little. Theodore having been told not to do a certain thing, persisted in doing it, Eleanor being engaged for a while with baby, he went on in the same way. As soon as E. was at liberty she said "Now Master Theodore, you know my rule?" He said "Yes"

"Then" said she "I must either punish you or break my word. If I break my word it will displease God. Now which am I to do? Do you wish me to keep my word and punish you or break it and displease God?" He at once went into the corner with the remark that she must not displease God, but he would be punished.

The day before this his nose having begun to bleed (this bleeding at the nose has been rather frequent since a fall which he had a few weeks ago upon his head in play and which at the time caused his nose to bleed profusely) his Mama wished to put a cold key down his back, a thing which some days before he refused to let her do. She said "I know Theodore, it will not be pleasant, but it will do you good. Now what am I to do" He at once replied "Just what you please Mama." His Mama improved this by observing that that was just what grownup people and children too should say to their Heavenly Father in all things. "Just what thou dost please my Father. Not my will but Thine be done." . . .

February 3rd, 1858
This morning, Theodore having said his prayers in much the usual manner, as Eleanor judged, remarked soon after that he did not feel happy. When asked why he said that he knew that when we prayed to God, we ought to speak from the heart, but he while saying his prayers had been thinking about Polly's doll's hat and he knew it was wrong and would like to say them over again. This was readily assented to and he knelt and repeated his prayers again, after which he said, putting his hand to his heart, he then felt much happier.

February 25th, 1858
Theodore's birthday. We have had a little party . . . and much have they enjoyed themselves . . . we have much pleasure in being able to record a marked improvement in our dear boy. His disposition is decidedly changed for the better . . . much of his improvement is attributable to the kind exertions of his new nurse (Eleanor) who is judicious in her treatment of the children as she is kind . . . His prayers now are not confined to a form, but he is encouraged to think of his own wants and to express them in his own language. We cannot fail to notice that he is increasingly affectionate. He is indeed *very* affectionate to his former nurse Jane and to Eleanor, as well as to his Papa and Mama, sister and baby. A little attention is beginning to be paid to his lessons, except when interrupted by outdoor exercise or other circumstances . . .

Basford House, Whalley Range, Manchester.[3]
May 24th, 1858
My very dear Boy, . . . While I am writing in the dining room I hear two of your cousins playing together upon the piano in the breakfast room. It is Ada and Lilly, she is called Lilly but her proper name is Elizabeth Esther. Evelyn is busy learning her lessons and Harry is in the loft over the coach house looking after his rabbits. He is going to have some Guinea-pigs and white mice – will not that be nice? He's a very good boy, so his Papa lets him have these things as a reward – and when you are old enough, if it should please God to let you live in this world to be as old as Harry, I daresay you will have some such nice things. Dear little Polly is in bed, I have just been up to see her. She was fast asleep and looked very nicely. Bless her. She and her little cousins Gertrude and Louise are very fond of each other and play nicely together. O that they may all love the Lord who bought them with his precious blood! . . . I told you in my last note about the peacock and peahen. Well, they are such rogues! . . . they . . . pick off the buds of the apple trees and cherry and plum trees and the strawberries and dig up the seeds. There will be hardly anything left to eat – so the naughty birds will have to be sent away and it will be a great pity – they are so pretty.

I spent a good deal of time in roaming through the fields and lanes looking for wild flowers and finding out their names like I do at home with you. But there are not many out yet – next month there will be plenty of them . . .

. . . Do you remember my dear boy, that God is your Father as well as mine. I want you to think of Him and love Him and try to please Him. You are his little boy and O He loves you more than I, though I love you very much . . .

Theodore and Mary in the 1850's

Samuel Mander's notebook

December 27th, 1858
Today our dear Polly's birthday has been celebrated with much innocent mirth

and glee. For some months past she, with Theodore and Geoffrey North (who has been staying with us since the end of September in consequence of the illness and death, the lamented death, of his dear Mama) has suffered from Hooping-cough. They have had it favourably and it has now nearly left them, but we have not thought it wise to invite their Cousins, or other little friends . . . as they could not have their Cousins they spent the day very happily with the Servants . . . Sarah the cook dressing them all up in great grandeur.

July 2nd, 1859 – *Theodore was 6*
. . . He continues affectionate and we hope truthful, though we have had on 1 or 2 occasions to doubt this. It was however more, we think, the result of inattention or inconsideration than of moral obliquity. He has been preserved from illness since our last notice. His health is good. We have lately had a set of Gymnastic apparatus fixed up chiefly for him and the use of which will, we hope, be beneficial.

O for guidance, divine guidance and help!

We must not longer omit to notice our dear little girl Ellen Beatrice who was born the 28th November last and has hitherto been remarkably healthy . . . From the age of about 2 months she has been put in her bassinette awake both night and day and has more frequently slept the whole of the night without waking than otherwise. We think she will be an amiable and gentle child, though this is of course a premature conjecture We receive it as a peculiar blessing that her health should have been so good while her dear Mama has been so much indisposed.

Our little Mima . . . is very healthy and has a good appetite. She is a funny little girl. Some months back she gained the name of "Sunshine" on account of her happy looking face. We have ceased to give her the name, as the showers seem quite as frequent as the sunshine; but for herself, she claims it still, "I Shiney" being the staple of her commentary on her own little self. We do not yet quite understand her character . . .

December 27th, 1859
Today dear Polly has made her appearance down stairs for the first time since Measles came on, about a week ago. She was much pleased with the Xmas tree, which was hung with little birthday presents from her various friends. As on her last birthday, the Hooping-cough prevented our visiting her little friends, so now did the Measles . . . Five lights sent forth their flickering rays around her birthday cake, in token of her years. This was in accordance with the German custom, as we learned from "Near Home" a book often read at the breakfast table.

February 25th, 1860
Our dear boy Samuel Theodore is 7 years old today. His uncle Charles has remembered it and has sent him an accordion and colour-box with which he is

much pleased. On the whole he is progressing nicely, with few exceptions. Slowness in everything – this is his characteristic failing. He too had the Measles last November.

Retrospective paragraph from Samuel Mander's notebook

At midsummer 1860 he went to Miss Reach's school as a daily boarder, staying during that quarter at his grandmama's. We then sent him as weekly boarder until Xmas. Not being very strong it was thought advisable that he should go with us to St. Leonards, where he continued till we left for Ryde.

At the start of that holiday Theodore began his first notebook

My notebook 1861

January 15. We all left home today. We saw ice in the fields. The sun shone very britly. The axle of our carriage broke but the guard saw it in time as we were going we saw Winsor castle, at last we got to our jornies end as we went to an Hotel and the lady was so funny and when we were going she filed our pokets with cakes so as we were going to Hastings we saw the Cristel Palace and the Hopyards. so at last we got to Hastings and we saw the sea and it looked so beautiful so that day we went a walk by the sea side

January 17. We walked in the country by a place called Bohemia.

January 18. Today Papa went to London to fetch Mama. We saw a soldiers funeral pass. first came some soldiers, then a band, then some riflemen, then some sailors, and at last came more soldiers the band played solemn music in going and a lively tune as they came back.

January 22. I rode out with Papa on Snowflake, a beautiful wite Pony.

January 24. Walked with Papa under the high cliffs on the E. side of Hastings. Saw some men at work in an iron-foundry making the moulds for casting the balustrade of a staircase

January 26. Polly, Mima and I drove out with Papa and Mama and saw some of the batteries on the coust called Martello towers.

February 20 and 21 heard two lectures on Japan and its Inhabitants

Retrospective record of 1861 holiday from Samuel Mander's notebook continued

His Uncle Charles coming over, we sent Theo back with him March 27, from St L to Miss Reach where he continued till Midsummer as full boarder. After the Midsummer holidays, he returned as weekly boarder but he remained only about 3 weeks, an attack of Dysentery rendering it necessary for him to be at home.

There is much about Theodore to please us. He is a child of a clear understanding, truthful and affectionate, of honest disposition and by no means deceptive. He has a tender conscience and generally seems very sorry when he does wrong. We are sorry to notice that idleness and inattention (frequently amounting to disobedience) are predominant features of his character. He is naturally very shy and unfriendly to strangers and backward in accosting them. This quality rather makes him dislike being a boarder at school, as he is not sufficiently free with his governess or sociable with his school-mates. He does not at present show much fondness for reading.

When a day has not been well spent it often happens that he is restless and cannot sleep till someone – usually his Mama – has prayed with him. He then generally becomes more composed and with a passage of scripture to think about, goes to sleep. He is a lively, cheerful boy and our prayer is that he may know the Lord and *so* know Him as to be preserved from the follies of youth.

Theodore's first notebook continued (1861)

December 3rd. Brother Benjamin was born

December 13th. Prince Albert died

December 23. He was buried at Windsor

December 25th. Had a very pretty Christmas tree

Samuel Mander's notebook

December 28
We are thankful to say that for the last 5 or 6 weeks, Theodore has been quite free from the Dysentery which lasted 3 months. On the 15th. October we took him to Leamington and had the advice of Dr. Sutherland, Home Physician and from that time he began to improve. We are now hoping that he will be well enough to return to school after the Xmas holidays. We desire to feel very thankful to God for His great goodness in this matter.

. . . At midsummer 1862 we removed him from Miss Reach's school to that of the Misses Tait and Townsend at Lytham, where he boarded for the first 6 months with Mr Thistlethwaite a tutor in the school. Not approving of this, we kept him at home the next quarter until he could be received into the school to board. During the quarter he was at home we found him very troublesome, being idle, dilatory etc. but when kept well employed he was a tolerably happy child. During his stay at Lytham we received fortnightly reports of his conduct, which were generally satisfactory.

Penn Fields, Wolverhampton. September 25th, 1862.
My very dear Boy,
. . . It has given me great pleasure to receive from your school mistresses reports on the whole so favourable. I hope you are trying every day to do your best in every way. That's the way for a boy to make progress and to be happy.

. . . Your Great Uncle Martin has been very ill but is now better again. I fear we shall not have him with us much longer.

. . . Do you remember Mr Day?[4] He is come over from America from the Northern States where the dreadful fighting is going on. He has lived many years in the state of Massachusetts at Boston where Benjamin Franklin was born. What a bloody and dreadful thing is man and especially war between inhabitants of the same country which is called "Civil War." Ask God to stop it soon and that this good may come out of it, that slavery may be quite done away with. You know, in America they say the poor black men have no souls, in fact are not men at all. Mr Day knows persons, even in the free states, who say the same and so they treat them just the same as they do cattle which is a shocking thing, for they have souls and minds and tender loving hearts like our own.

Do you walk out much and on the shore? I want you to walk a great deal and run and jump and climb etc. Anything but being lazy. I hope you are happy. Mama and I hope to go over to see you soon. I pray for you every day and I do not doubt God's goodness to you.

Goodbye, your affectionate father, Samuel S. Mander

Wolverhampton April 22nd, 1863
My dear Boy,
And so you wish me to ask you some questions . . .

Well now:- Question 1 What were the names of the Roman emperors who, before the Christian era (and) first after it, invaded Britain?

Question 2 Who is the *meekest* man mentioned in the Bible? Who is the most *patient* and who the most *loving*? . . . Last night your dear Mama and I called at your Uncle Francis'. He had been out for the day on one of his Botanizing Excursions. He and the gentlemen who were with him visited Bromsgrove – Lickey, a lofty hill, which you will find marked on a good map, in

Worcestershire. They found no fewer than 60 different plants, all more or less in bloom which at this early part of wild flower time is a very great many. I should have liked to go with them but I was prevented by public business. Now "on public business" almost always has to do with keeping or doing good and to the said public, which means your neighbours and it is right to attend to this is it not? . . .

May 28th, 1863
My dear Boy,
Mima's letter was received and read by us all. You say you received a letter from me from Amsterdam? – did you not receive one also from Antwerp or Brussels? I wrote you from one of those places, I forget which. Let me know in your next letter. I send you a few stamps, they are only what we receive ourselves. I cannot get any more for you from other places. Polly and Mima are enjoying themselves very much at Aunt Nelly(s) Miss Garett has left us so they have no lessons just now.

Now for some questions:-

1 Against what peoples or nations did Edward 1st. fight?
2 Which is the flattest country in Europe and which is the most mountainous?
3 How long were the Jews in captivity in Babylon?

There, I think you will do those easily – though it is not everyone who could answer the questions.

Goodbye, my time is gone, with much love, your affectionate Papa.

The following letter written in copperplate doubled as a school report and as an example of Theodore's best writing.

Lytham December 7th, 1863
My dear Papa,
We hope to come home on Thursday the 17th instant, we shall leave Lytham by the 11.45 train due in Manchester at 2.10. One of the ladies will take charge of me as usual, if you will kindly meet me at the Victoria Station.

Miss Tait and Miss Townsend desire their kind regards and hope you will be pleased with my progress this half year. I have written to the end of the fifty fourth exercise in "Arnolds first Latin Book." I have construed and parsed "Sentences in Prose and Verse" in Delectus and perfected many of the Syntax rules. Our English lessons have included English and Roman History, Geography, Grammar and writing from dictation: in Arithmetic I am working practice. We have written many abstracts from History and common objects. Our Scripture lessons have been as usual repeating daily texts and reading from the Old and New Testament, morning and evening. This is the last letter you will receive from me this half year. I am quite well. With best love to all, I remain dear Papa, your affectionate son, S. Theo M.

Theodore aged about 10

Retrospective report on Theodore from Samuel Mander's notebook

Finding him still continue (sic) delicate we felt anxious to have him nearer home, especially as little attention seemed to be paid to physical training and the Tettenhall Proprietary School being now opened, we wished to remove him there before the House was full, and so on the 1st. of April 1864 we sent him there.[5] On leaving Lytham, Miss Tait spoke very favourably of him and in a letter written afterwards she said "I am sure Theo will be beloved of his new instructors, if only they get to understand him: he is so very shy and undemonstrative with strangers, that very little of his real character and capabilities can be known for some time." He has now been at Tettenhall about 6 months as a weekly boarder. He continues to look delicate.

That entry of October 10th, 1864 is the last one in Samuel Mander's notebook on his children.

1865 – 1873

Ridler's Hotel, Holborn, London. May 9th, 1865
My dear Theodore,
We left Paris on Saturday evening, spent a quiet and very pleasant Sunday at Dieppe, sailed from there on Monday morning and got here about 5 pm after a very smooth passage, Polly not being at all sick or any such. Your dear Mama wants to see a little more of London and so I propose staying here until Friday next, seeing some of the many very interesting things that are to be seen here and returning home on that day. On Saturday therefore, if all be well, you will go home and I hope we may have the great pleasure of meeting you in good health with a smiling face . . .

Queen's Hotel, Bristol. March 11th, 1866
My very dear Boy,
. . . I can't help thinking sometimes how fast your school days are going by. Well never mind if you're making good use of the time . . . I want you to be a good boy. Remember that, in answer to your prayers and your dear Mama's and mine. God does send you, give you, His Holy Spirit. He speaks to you by a little gentle voice within. And this voice it is in your power to disregard and disobey. But Oh, if I could only say one more sentence to you it should be "don't do so, but listen and obey." Then sweet singing will be heard in your heart . . . I remain, my dear boy, your affectionate father, Samuel S. Mander.

Theodore's notebook[6] 1866, he was 13

Passed the Cambridge examination, without honours.

1867
Began to teach in the Sunday Infants' School, Wolverhampton with Robert Horton.

February 17th, 1867
Papa gave me an airgun for passing the examination.
Began to take walks with Mr White to learn Natural History.

February 23rd.
Cousin Mander married

1868
January 3rd.
We all went to Bournemouth for the winter, took riding lessons, it's a beautiful place. One gets the country with many fir woods and heaths close by the sea. There are not many shells to be found there.

Letter addressed to Mrs Mander, Hastings House, Bournemouth. Hants

Tettenhall March 11th, 1868
My Dear Mama,

Thank you for your letter. We had a half holiday on Monday for the Bishop, at least he asked for it.

The boys went hare and hounds for about 14 miles. Papa has offered some prizes next Christmas for the best readers and writers.

Today is very wet and so we cannot go out.

Last Sunday I went to Aunt Nellie's to dinner and to tea. That hole in my trousers has been mended. I always ride or drive to and from school . . . my new boots do very well. Can I wear my new boots every day with the others because . . . I do not get these I am wearing now cleaned every day.

A new boy named Smith came today. Dr. Thomas brought him. We have a great deal of work to do now. I shall be very glad when you come home.

The cellars at Glen Bank are being roofed over. I am very happy I have given my heart to God. There is not much to say so with much love to all, I remain your affectionate son, S.T. Mander.

Holiday notebook

Spring 1868 A journey to Holland
Start from Wolverhampton at 7.30. A four hour and a half journey to London. Pass through the Black country also past . . . Baron Rothschild's residence. Get into Euston station . . . to Epsom to see Mary who was very happy. At 4.35 back again to London . . . Reached Harwich almost 12 am. Got on board the steamer (Zealous) at 1 am, start for Rotterdam. A very calm night. Passed many lighthouses and a lightship . . . Saw the phosphorus on the water by the paddle wheels beautifully. Went to sleep on deck for an hour; went downstairs and had another hour and a half. The sailors caught some fish and hung them on the inside of the ship . . . A sail was spread out over the deck for a shade from the wind . . . Crossed the bar at the mouth of the Maas, a sand bank. Stop and sound, 18 feet. Not enough, go back and wait. Go on again . . . 11 o'clock, pilot

and custom officers come on board. Landed 1 pm.

. . . Saw many curious things: looking glass outside the windows to see who passes along the road, markets of little round Dutch cheeses, dogs drawing carts of bright brass milk cans, people wearing large wooden boots, women[7] with horns of brass wire on each side of their faces, gentlemen wear white trousers, doors in rooms are made just like the rest of the walls so you can scarcely tell they are there.

Rotterdam is full of ships, canals everywhere, large and deep; its water is not good for foreigners who have therefore to drink Seltzer water. Saw . . . the corn exchange (a fine building) and the cathedral, the park and Zoological gardens. Went on board two merchantmen with cargoes of sugar and coffee from Java. 6.30 started for Delft. Saw new church with monuments to William 1 and Grotius . . . also the house in which William 1 was assassinated, it is called the Prinsenhof . . . Delft is a very pretty clean place with canals and avenues of trees like Rotterdam.

From Delft Theodore and his father travelled to the Hague where they visited the art gallery and a number of public buildings

. . . Thence we drove to Leyden . . . We stayed at the Lion d'Or. Many houses in Holland are built with curious high gable ends towards the roads . . . The poor women are very clean dressed in a blue jacket coming below their waists . . . wooden sabots and white caps, sometimes with long earrings . . . The bricks in Holland are mostly very small, almost all the streets are paved . . . Many women wear immense hats for carrying baskets on.

They stayed overnight in Haarlem and visited Broek and Zaandam

. . . We drove a large part of the way on a high dyke. Came back to Amsterdam by steamer. Went to Alkmaar . . . Then to the Helder . . . saw two large ships, one a steamer made in England with a revolving turret on which was a cannon, the other a large man of war which served as a naval school for several hundred boys. Returned next morning and passed through . . . Amsterdam . . . and Rotterdam then by steamer to Harwich 1 pm to 1 am next morning; then to London and home again.

Theodore's diary

Took up our abode at Glen Bank[8] leaving old Penn Fields September 1868

1869, Brother Bertram (Martin) born June 5th.

Howard began school life

Went to Dijon for a year July 8th.

Rue Fontaine, Dijon. July 12, 1869.

My very dear Mama,

I have now been here nearly five days and have seen the whole place with Papa; he started for Paris last night or rather this morning at 12.13. This is a very nice place; there is a wood about a mile from our house, it is called the Park and is very pleasant to walk in during this hot weather. There is a small river, which being damned (sic) up makes a beautiful place for bathing and rowing. There are baths and boats there. There are some very pretty gardens nearer to us called the "Jardins des Arquebuses." There are also several large old Roman Catholic churches in the town. We saw a little of the service in two of them yesterday. The Dukes of Burgundy had a palace here, part of which is now a museum and another part of Mr Perluzon's chapel. We have been to see the cemetery most of the graves appear to be those of Catholics, many of them very much decorated, but the whole place is kept very badly. One evening we drove to Plombiere, a village a little way from Dijon. We found several new plants and as we returned in the twilight we caught two glow-worms; as Papa will tell you, we could almost see to read by their light.

I have no one to speak to but in French now so I think I shall get on well, at any rate I ought and shall try to. Mr Perluzon says I know French well enough to begin my lessons with Mr Dudrumel who will be my master this week, and also German with a German lady who speaks French like a native.

Will you settle with Papa what musical instrument you would like me to learn and let me know. If I learn the piano I shall have to hire one but both Mr and Mrs Perluzon think that would be better than the violin because the violin is so difficult. It is exceedingly hot here now, a hotter summer than they have had for some time. Papa has bought me a kind of Panama hat which is very cool.

How are you all? How is Martin? Has he been registered yet? I hope someone will write to me soon. You see, I am one and you are many so I ought to have more letters than you.

It is a great blessing to have Jesus to speak to at any time and to tell everything to. Without him I should be very unhappy but as it is I am very happy except a curious feeling which will soon pass away.

I think Mr and Mrs Perluzon are going to see some friends at Beaune, a town perhaps an hour away by train from here. They will take me with them. When are Mary and Mima going to Blackpool?

With very much love to you, Papa and all. I remain my dear Mama, your very affectionate son S.T. Mander

P.S. Papa has been complemented many times on his very good French.

Rue de Fontaine, Dijon. July 19th, 1869
My very dear Mama,

It is Papa's turn to have a letter but I must answer your questions.

My room is on the third story and I don't know what rooms are next to it. I never go into them. I don't think they all belong to Mr Perluzon. I think some of them are for other boys if any come. The rest of our rooms are on the second story; there is a garden at the back divided between the different tenants of this house and the next; we have a little summer house in which I sometimes learn my lessons; just by is the pigeon house. Mr P. has between 20 and 30 pigeons. I think I would rather learn the violin. Mr Perluzon says the noise will not matter if I practise in my bedroom. There is a good teacher, I think he charges 2 francs a lesson. I don't like to ask about practising on their piano but I daresay I shall be able to sometimes. It is very hot here. I do not dress specially for dinner. My address is as follows:-

S.T. Mander, Mons. le Pasteur Perluzon, Rue de Fontaine, Dijon. Cote d'Or. With much love to yourself and all the others I remain your very affectionate son Theodore.

Rue de Fontaine. August 16th, 1869
My very dear Mama,

I have plenty of letters. I have had one from Mr Felkin[9] and one from Mr North. I have written to Willie Smyth, but he has not written to me; if you have a chance will you let him know that I very much want a letter from him. I have also written to Charlie and Robert. I write about 2 letters a week, that is 8d.

Thank you very much for what you say in your letter about the pocket money but I would rather not have any more . . .

Yesterday (Sunday) was the Emperor's fete here and throughout France.

I am almost sure we are not going to Switzerland; perhaps we shall go somewhere here for a short week but I think that will be all . . . I shall be very glad when I can preach like John Shaw[10]. I have such temptations in my mind; such questions as these present themselves. How do I know there is a God? How do I know there is a Saviour? I have never seen Him. How do I know the Bible is true? It has been like this today and for a day or two except yesterday afternoon. And I cannot pray easily. And my faith is weak. May God sustain me. Please pray for me and write to me.

With *very* much love, Theodore – but God is very good to give me joy at all, besides these times I have also very happy times.

Theodore 1869

Rue de Fontaine, Dijon. September 13th, 1869
My very dear Mama,

. . . I am much happier now; my desire and I think my duty, is to prepare to enter Papa's business, as you say and I think I can be quite as useful in that way as being a minister. I think God has led Papa to find the best place he could have done for me. The more I am with M. Perluzon the more I see he is a good, earnest and useful man . . .

I am well occupied all day now; I translate Latin whenever I have time and

I shall read it to Mr Dudrumel once a week, taking ½ an hour from one of the other lessons for it. Almost every evening I take a walk with M. Peluzon. He is going through with me all the differences between the Protestant and Catholic religions, telling me all their doctrines and refuting them all by proofs from the Bible . . .

Some times I take a walk with Lucien Dudrumel; I have had some religious talk with him; he is Catholic by name but nothing at heart. He is exceedingly thoughtless and dark as a heathen on the subject of Religion. He never reads the Bible and has scarcely ever seen it. I have tried to persuade him to be more thoughtful and to get out of the great danger he is in but he does not seem now much to care whether he is saved or lost. He says he must enjoy himself now during his youth.

Madame Perluzon often buys things on Sunday for dinner and I scarcely like to eat them. Is it wrong to eat them? I often read a French book to Madame P. for ½ an hour or an hour in the afternoon or evening. She has a book of meditations and prayers which I generally read to her in the evening with a chapter of the Bible . . .

Can I have, when you send the other things, a book, a nice English poetry. It is so dark I cannot see lines now. Often I feel sorrowful but when I think of Jesus I feel happy again.

With much love to you and all I remain your very affectionate Theodore.

Rue de Fontaine, Dijon. October 18th, 1869
My very dear Mama,

I write the French letters very nearly as quickly as the English and I do not use the dictionary. We have had pretty warm weather hitherto but this morning at 6 o'clock my thermometer showed 3 degrees below freezing point and some water that I put out last night was all frozen. I have had a fire in my stove for the first time this morning. It warms the room very nicely. Please to thank Nellie and Lottie very much for their letters. I should so like to see you all! . . . You do not say in your letter whether I can try a velocipede. Will you send me Howard's address please.

My chain broke one day and my watch fell on some stones which broke a wheel inside; it has gone to be mended.

I have been obliged to buy a new felt hat.

I do not feel any want of a dress coat; I am wearing almost all my clothes in turn, but principally my grey ones; my best black ones I have only worn three or four times.

. . . I should so like to see Martin!

. . . If the violin does nothing else it teaches me to keep my temper and to be patient.

. . . I suppose the Tettenhall boys have begun to collect wood for the bonfire. How are our gardens? Please to tell Mary and Mima not to cut the bulbs in digging; there are a good many of them and they will look very pretty in the spring . . .

Now with very much love to you and all, I remain always your very loving son, Theodore.

Rue de Fontaine, Dijon. January 3rd 1870
My very dear Mama,

. . . Papa told me I could buy things with discretion, so I have bought a book on heat (2 fr.) and I sent to Paris at the same time that M.P. was sending, for a Physical Geography of the world (6 fr.) highly recommended by M.P. and others . . . How delightful it will be to come home again; I've been half my time on Thursday. Have you killed the pigs? How much did they weigh? Thank you for the cards; they are very nice and remind me much of old England . . .

January 1870
. . . I have had my teeth attended to . . . I spent 3 ½ pleasant hours at the dentist's. He filed and sawed and scraped and bored. After that he stopped 5 with gold. And the large and bad one he stopped with mastic, and with a piece of platinum underneath because it bled. Now they are all done and well done and comfortable. M.P. and I thought it was better to have it done with gold, because it is, so to speak, a life long thing. Gold can be taken out if they ache, and with it the teeth keep their colour; with the other thing which is a mixture of silver and tin, they turn grey and it often cannot be taken out when they ache . . .

That is about all I have to say, so with very much love to yourself and Papa, Aunt Fraser and all, I remain ever, your very affectionate son Theodore

Glen Bank, Wolverhampton. January 18 1870
My dear Theodore,

I send you today a newspaper containing a speech by Mr W.E. Foster (sic) our minister of Education on the various matters now stirring the mind of the country. The period of your stay at Dijon may justly be called one of the most important in the annals of England. After the Irish question, comes that of English Education, one of supreme importance. Two societies have taken up the question before defending the sides into which English life is divided on almost all questions, the stand-stills and the progressives. The latter took the field first and have pushed forward their battalions with surprising ardour. They constitute the "National Education League" which seeks to secure the education of *every* child in the land, using compulsion if necessary, having *free* schools, supported partly by national grants and partly by local rates, the schools to be *entirely* (non) *sectarian* ie – teaching none of the peculiarities of any sect. This League alarmed the Clergy of the Establishment and another league was quietly founded to cope with it, called the "National Education Union" To this belong almost all the clergy and almost all the Tory party. A grand struggle is expected but may be that, as Mr Foster says, the Government have a plan which will give pretty general satisfaction . . .

How great, how wonderful, how high are the mysteries of Redeeming love. That God should take the nature of his fallen rebellious Creature and be Divine . . . If we admit Him to our hearts He becomes our strength for obedience, our (January 20th.- I was unable to finish on the 18th.) guide for service or as the apostle puts it "He of God is made to us wisdom . . ." without Him we are nothing, can do nothing . . . He desires free love, willing service and obedience. Your Aunt Fraser has been much better but is worse again I am sorry to say. She is still with us. Goodbye, with much love, your affectionate father, Samuel Mander.

Theodore's notebook and diary

1870
Went to Switzerland with Monsieur and Madame Perluzon and Vere Smith.
Smith and I took a week's tour from . . . Geneva by Neuchatel etc . . .
August. Returned to Tettenhall School.

Christmas. Passed Cambridge senior exam with honours. Distinguished in French.

Natural history notebook

Having procured an owl I keep him in a darkened cot, with liberty to fly about in a small aviary at night

When I approach him with my hand, he pecks at it, and leaning back, throws forward his feet to catch it.

His claws are very sharp.

March 11. Gave my owl a dead mouse. After looking at it intently for 5 or 10 minutes, and knocking his nose against it, he took it in his bill, and swallowed it whole in about half a dozen gulphs (sic) He has a habit of bending his head down, when he is approached, and rolling it thus from side to side, he gives his feet an occasional tap with his beak.

March 14. Found a pellet about ½ in. diam. in the owl's cot. Upon examination I found it to consist of a part of the bones and fur of the mouse he had swallowed on the 11th.

April 4. Owl swallowed a hen brown linnet whole, after some difficulty.

In 1871 several letters were received by Samuel Mander all containing suggestions for the next step in Theodore's education

Elberfeld. March 5th. 1871
Dear Sir,

In reply to your favour of the 1st. inst. I have pleasure of informing you of the details in question.

I should not advise your son to attend the school in which I teach, because it would not answer your purpose so well. But there is a special college for studying chemistry conducted by Mr Artope on exactly the same plan as that of Dr. Fresnius at Wiesbaden. It has a laboratory in which the students may spend as many hours as they like: besides, there are lectures proceeding from the elementary to the most advanced instruction. Elberfeld, being a large manufacturing town, many sorts of manufacturers attend this college in order to acquire knowledge necessary for the various branches of business. In a school connected with this college your son might attend lessons of German every day and of other subjects if desired. Mr Artope, whom I know well, is a clever and amiable man, and would take much interest in your son's progress. His terms are £15 a year, including chemicals used in the laboratory with the exception of silver platina and the like.

We should be able to give your son a nice airy bedroom where he might also sit in the day when wishing to be alone. I should make him read and write German and study the grammar and he would of course join our conversation. Mrs K. speaks German very well and if he would make it a rule not to talk English I think she would not induce him to break it. She might explain difficulties to him when I am not at home and help him on much colloquial German. The society of some lads living in our family would be profitable in the same way. In the autumn holidays (five weeks in all schools) we generally take a journey. We should like you to arrange matters accordingly, perhaps you might take a trip too. I should expect your son to follow my directions respecting the employment of his time but would gladly allow him as much liberty as consistent with my responsibility. There are good and earnest preachers here, whose sermons he certainly would find very useful.

Our terms for board and lodging and instruction (except Mr Artope's) would be seventy pounds a year, paid quarterly in advance. This would not include washing which I believe is cheaper than in England. The next term at the college begins soon after Easter, but you might send your son sooner if you prefer it.

I am dear sir, Yours truly,
M. Krummachen

Letter written by Henry Felkin from Germany, to his brother, Robert Felkin, on March 12th 1871

. . . Now the real object of my letter, viz. Theodore Mander's want of a general school etc. I have had an hour's talk with my friend and neighbour Prof. Newbold . . . first the language. The purest and best general is undoubtedly spoken in Hanöver and the next best in Brunswick. The Berlin accent is horrid . . . I think you exaggerate the importance of this, or rather Mr Mander does. Where ever Theodore learns it (the language) if he stays 10 years he will never lose the foreign accent and educated people will know within a few minutes conversation that he is an Englishman, while if Theodore is moderately careful they need never know where he has learnt his German . . . The first technical institution in Germany is the Dresden . . . school and a first rate one too. The next is our Chemnitz one. The Ruhr academy is also a splendid . . . institution.

In Carlsruhe there is also a Polytechnic school of the first class as also in Heidelburg . . . The Elberfeld one I cannot hear everything about . . . You see the difficulty is not to find a school but to chose one . . .

Letter from Henry Felkin to Samuel Mander

Chemnitz 25 March 1871
My Dear Sir,

I duly received your letter with its enclosures yesterday and late today consulted my friend Prof. Newbold on the subject.

He seems quite of opinion that Theodore is sufficiently advanced to enter the 2nd. class . . . His principal anxiety seemed to be that T. should have so much knowledge of German and of German technical terms, expressions and words as to enable him to understand what is taught orally in class. He wished me at once to buy and send him per post, a German chemical work – a work in the German language by Fresnius . . . for him to begin studying *at once* that he may accustom himself to the German technical expressions. I will send the work tomorrow per post as under any circumstances it will be useful to him . . .

My brother may not perhaps have mentioned that we are moving next week from our present abode and this, I much regret, will prevent us offering you and Theodore a room. My wife and I feel quite grieved that it just so happens, we should have liked to have had you as our guests, we hope however that you will give us all your spare time and spend the evenings with us. It is so seldom that English friends come it is quite a treat to us . . .

5 Crescent Place, Clapham Common. March 27 1871

My dear Cousin,

My opinion is unaltered that it would really be worth all the extra time involved for Theodore to matriculate well at the London University. The examination is not generally looked upon as a simple one. I believe it is admitted to be more trying than the preliminary ones at Oxford and Cambridge. After having passed it an undergraduate can at once proceed to study for the B.A. for which 2 exams are held. You will see from the calendar that Henry passed the 1st. B.A. exam in the June or July following the January in which he matriculated . . . If a man wishes to take a degree at the London University he *must* matriculate of course but of the hundreds that go up for this exam but a small proportion ever intend going further, they go up solely for the benefit that a study for it gives them and also for the credit they having passed it well, will receive from society . . .

I cannot see any objection beyond the delay in going abroad, this I feel sure will be fully compensated. I think you intend placing Theodore after his return from abroad with some London firm. I expect you will find then, that the University certificate will be of use.

His cousin Charles will be a Cambridge man and Theodore, I hope, a London undergraduate at least. I have given my opinion fully, as you were kind enough to do me the honour, shall I say, of asking me . . .

With kindest love to Cousin Mary and yourself . . . Believe me my dear Cousin, Yours affectionately, J. Spencer Pearsall.

Extract from a letter from J. D. Heard of the Religious Tract Society to Samuel Mander 1871

. . . I can confidently recommend Zurich . . . where the Laboratory etc . . . is first rate . . . The students board out with professors etc. A professor at Wellington College, a Swiss, is about to settle in Zurich with one or two pupils and I can confidently recommend him as a young man of good morals and excellent character if you wish to entrust your son to him. He is the son of a Prussian cavalry officer who fought at Waterloo, his mother is still living and it is to provide a home for her that he is about to return to Zurich where she resides . . .

Tettenhall Proprietary School, report for the half year ending midsummer 1871

Name – Mander S.T. Form V
Number of boys in Form – 6
French .... Place in Form – 1 Very good.
Arithmetic/Algebra etc ...... Place in Form – 2 Very fair

English Literature	Place in Form – 3 Satisfactory
Geography	Place in Form – 3 Satisfactory
Chemistry	Place in Form – 1 Very good

Notebook

Botanical Tour in Switzerland. July 4 '71
Tuesday
At 8.50 am Uncle Fraser[11], Rev. J. Thompson and I left Wolverhampton for London and Harwich. And as the faces of the dear ones I left behind faded in the distance, sad misapprehensions filled my mind of dangers that might befall me during my absence, and I knew that perhaps I was looking on these dear figures for the last time this side eternity. But as I remembered that God can guard *all* His family here below, and that His eye continually rests on every individual of it, I felt reassured, and my manifold fears were dissipated.

After a hot and tedious journey we reached Harwich at 3.40 pm. We went immediately on board the steamer destined to convey us to Rotterdam; Mr Thompson and I employed the interval before starting in inspecting the vessel and in taking in provisions for the journey. When we had started and got out from land, we found the German Ocean rather rough, and our boat rolled and pitched most disagreeably. We then began to fear for the safety of the provision of food we had laid in, and alas! our fears were only too correctly realised, for within an hour or two from leaving land we were as empty as before we started and perhaps more so. Uncle Fraser had taken in nothing, although he did experience that peculiarly delightful sensation called squeamishness.

I secured a mattress downstairs, but Uncle F. and Mr T. preferred the floor on deck to the idea of a search (which they supposed hopeless) for a bed of some kind below boards. At 4.30 am (July 5) I woke and came on deck and at once perceived the sandhills and soon after the windmills of the Dutch coast.

From Rotterdam they travelled by train to Cologne

. . . Went immediately to see the cathedral so justly renowned. It is a fine pile of building and when finished will be, I suppose, the finest structure of its kind in Europe. The two large towers in front, intended to be 500 feet high, are at present only about half finished, though the building was begun in 1248 . . . it contains some very beautiful painted glass windows. For a little more than 4 francs we were shown the relics; among which the most striking were the heads of the three Magi and 2 or 3 links of the chain by which Peter was confined in prison. We also visited the church of St Ursula, an old place where among other relics are the bones of 11,000 virgins who came over *long ago* from England with

St Ursula. Also two thorns out of the crown of Christ and one of the stone water pots of Cana, which I had the pleasure of holding in my hand . . . Next morning July 6 we had started for Basel by 6 o'clock . . . The Rhine valley from Bonn to Mainz is very beautiful . . . and as one passes along, one ruined castle after another comes into sight, perched on the tops of hills overlooking the river . . . On arriving at Mainz the most picturesque part of the Rhine ceases, the mountains retire further from the river, and the plain is covered with vine yards, cornfields, tobacco plantations etc. All the way from Rotterdam the fields were remarkable as having no hedges; in Holland the deficiency was supplemented by ditches and canals but here as in many parts of France there were no such marks of division at all . . . arrived in Basel after a 14 hours ride. Travelling on the continent often seems tedious and long to an Englishman, who in his own small island is accustomed to reckon 4 or 6 hours a long journey, especially as the trains run much more slowly than in England. On arriving in Basel we had travelled continuously for 3 days having accomplished rather more than 800 miles. When we had tea and done some writing we were ready for bed, and therefore retired without loss of time to gain fresh strength for another day's travel.

After breakfast – July 7 – next morning, we took a stroll into the town, and obtained a very good view of it from the middle of the bridge over the Rhine, with its cathedral and its lofty houses rising up from the very edge of the river; it looked very picturesque . . .

Leaving Basel at ten we started on our way to Coire. We made the time pass agreeably by looking over our bill, settling our affairs in a new money, and talking to our fellow passengers in French, with grand attempts also at German. Two soldiers returning from the war were in our carriage. One of them had five decorations among which the "Iron Cross" was conspicuous. The other told us that 20 cavalry had charged at him and wounded him, and he shewed two sabre cuts in his forehead. We also amused ourselves by reading different notices for the benefit of travellers, such as "In diesen coupe wird man nicht rauchen" shewing characteristic politeness as compared with the English "No smoking allowed" . . .

At Constance we had more than an hour to spare, and spent that time in looking at the town, inspecting the cathedral, buying a thermometer and a prism, and in seeing the Hall of the Kaufhaus in which the Great Council of Constance held its sittings. It was that famous assembly that condemned John Huss[12] and Jerome of Prague. We saw in a room above this Hall, a model of the dungeon in which Huss was confined with the actual door and other fragments incorporated in it. It is exceedingly small, I should say 6 feet by 2 feet and 5 feet high. It is the same size as the original was . . .

Quitting Constance . . . we travelled down the valley of the Rhine which at the time was flooded and so we had to proceed slowly and cautiously; for a few days before part of the railway had been carried away by the stream . . . We arrived in Coire at 10 pm . . .

July 8

Obliged to be up again at 4 o'clock, we leave Coire at 4.45 without any breakfast. The large diligence being full we had to find places in a supplementary vehicle of a smaller and less business-like description. At first travelling was rather tedious, but when we arrived at Thusis a short stay was made for a relay of horses, so we ran on and obtained a view of the entrance of the "Via Mala." It was very grand and promised very awful scenery for the interior which unhappily we had no time to see, for our coach soon came up, and we ran a narrow chance of being left behind. The scenery now became generally very splendid . . . The road passed along the edges of dreadful precipices, at the bottom of which roared the wild mountain torrent. Here and there the road is covered to protect it from avalanches, which are now very frequent on account of the heat.

. . . in an hour or two's time we . . . enter the Julier Pass. The first part is all up hill work and the coach travels at walking pace, so we are able to botanize for two or three hours bringing our plants in every now and then. At last we arrive at the top of the Pass amongst the snow, then no more botanizing, for we descend quickly and after one more relay of horses and change of coaches . . . we soon arrive at our destination, viz St Moritz, after 13 hours travelling . . .

Sunday July 9

Our headquarters are 3 bedrooms together on the second floor of the Veraguth Hotel, thence we proceed on Sunday morning to the parish church, a curious place, with uncomfortable narrow wooden seats, a pretty new little organ, high pulpit, collection boxes placed on tables at the doors, and texts written up round the building in Romansch. Being very early . . . went out, distributed a few tracts, and made the people read German and French to us, taking sections either out of the tracts or out of the Bible . . . Five languages are spoken in this village, German, Romansch, Italian, French and English; and many of the inhabitants can speak 3 or 4 of them.

. . . St Moritz is very prettily situated near the southern end of the Haute Engadine . . . Below us lies quiet and tranquil, a . . . lake whose waters are of a deep green colour, which seems peculiar to these elevated mountain lakes . . . And above us the blue sky displays that depth of colour so well known to Italian travellers. It is a very beautiful place, and is a good type of Swiss mountain scenery.

July 10
. . . the country round here affords a fruitful field for botanical research. After having some very good finds, we return to dinner which takes place every day at 12.30. In the afternoon . . . Mr T. and I occupy ourselves . . . with the drying and pressing of our plants.

July 11
Start at 7 am for the mountain on the other side of the lake intending to return at dinner time. But we meet with such success in the botany line that dinner becomes quite a secondary consideration, and we determine to go without it for once. We ascend as far as the snow and then it begins to rain and we begin to descend, coming down through the woods behind the Kurhaus, which is a chalybeate[13] water establishment. It is much frequented by people from different parts, who drink the water, which tastes something like lemonade, and also take baths in it. We arrive at our hotel at 4 having been away nine hours with half a bun each to eat. We spent the evening again in arranging our treasures.

During the next few days they continued to botanize and to visit places nearby

July 17
Went by coach to Pontresina. Our coach was full inside, so we had a romantic ride on the top among the luggage. The apparent inconvenience became an advantage, as our position afforded us a splendid view of the Engadine and its mountains. An hour and a half brought us to Pontresina and when we had dined, we took a carriage and visited the glacier of Mortiratch. Having never seen a glacier before, I was much surprised by its appearance. It filled a narrow valley, extending back perhaps 10 miles to a mountain totally covered with snow . . . We went upon it, and crossed several small crevasses. In the very front, at the point where the river issues from beneath the moving mass, a large piece of ice had fallen, forming an archway, and shewing its real colour to be green. When we had botanized for a short time in the environs, we returned to Pontresina where we stayed the night.

July 18
Took a carriage directly after breakfast to the Val de Fain, a very elevated valley in the direction of the Bernina range. At the entrance of the valley we took refreshment in a little "auberge." It was a long, low house built partly of wood; the back floors were made simply of trees laid side by side in their rough state.

The "aubergiste" gave us butter, honey, and quince preserve with our bread and coffee. It seems to be the custom always to take honey as well as butter, with bread throughout Switzerland. Our repast at an end, we started up the valley on foot, our driver carrying our bags, vasculum etc. This valley offered very good ground for botanical research and we found consequently many good flowers . . . as we advanced the snow increased. At one time we saw a marmot standing on a rock . . . but when it perceived us it darted into its hole . . . A little further on we came upon an Italian who possessed the only cottage we saw all the time; he was feeding cows and mules and at our request which was made thus, "un poco late" and which he immediately understood whether right or wrong, he brought up a cow and milked it on the spot, supplying us with a warm fresh drink.

Soon after this we got into the snow, and had also to cross a small river of ice-cold water. Mr Th. and I took off our shoes and stockings and crossed barefoot, but finding this a more unpleasant than economical mode of procedure we put on our boots and pocketed our stockings . . . Returning we had to traverse more than a mile of snow broken here and there by small islands of rock. Then came the river. Mr Th. and I waded it with our boots on and were almost thrown down in the middle by the force of the current. Uncle Fraser and the guide more wisely went on a little further and found a snow bridge, some 20 ft. high. After a ten mile walk (altogether) . . . we regained our inn at Pontresina in time for a six o'clock Table d'hote, after which we took the same carriage and man as before, having become rather friendly with him, and arrived at St Moritz about 8 or 9 pm. The driver was highly pleased with a 5 fr. "Trink-geld" for his day's trouble.

July 20

Hired a "Zwei-spanner" with a very agreeable driver to transport us and our luggage over the Maloggia Pass to Chiavenna. We might have been very important persons (as perhaps we were) from the farewell we received. The masters, waiters, chambermaids, and many of the visitors came to the door to shake hands and see us off. What with this, and looking after luggage and distributing francs in diverse directions we were some time in getting off. But we did start at last and a beautiful drive we had.

. . . For several hours the mountains rose around us to a great height in bold grandeur, some presenting jagged summits, others rounder and with a little snow still remaining upon them . . . Pretty waterfalls peeped out now and then from their dark recesses. Huge rocks in some parts strewed the plain, which had fallen from the neighbouring mountains. In two places we saw where a village had been destroyed by some of these landslips. The village of Pleurs was destroyed with 2,030 inhabitants in 1648 . . . At length we arrived in Chiavenna, a quaint old Italian town, with narrow dirty streets and a great many churches . . . It was very hot here, and we found it very pleasant to walk about outside after dark; in fact Mr Th. and I stayed up till after 11 to watch the arrival of one of Cook's parties conducted by Mr Ripley, his manager. They were travelling from

Coire to Milan by diligence, and only stayed half an hour to take tea.

The following day they sailed to Porlezza on Lake Lugano

. . . we took tea in the open air by the lake while our luggage was placed in a boat. When we had finished tea and had got rid of the numerous "facini" I think they are called, who bothered for money, we started on a romantic sail across the lake. It lasted about 3 hours, the men standing up and pushing instead of pulling their oars . . . Towards the end of our row the moon and stars came out and the effect was very beautiful. We arrived late at Lugano and there went to the Hotel Washington which is within a few yards of the lake.

On July 22 travelling by carriage and steamer they arrived in Stresa

. . . The rest of the day was spent in arranging our plants at the "Hotel des Iles Borromees" and in writing my diary and in dining at Table d'hote. It is necessary to mention the dining, for it took a very long time, there were so many courses.

July 24 Monday
Started at 6 am by steamboat for Maggalino, and arrived there after a beautiful sail of 3 or 4 hours. Took the diligence immediately for Bellinoza. The ride was flat and I went to sleep . . . Bellinoza is the chief town of the canton of . . . Ticino . . . This is the only canton in which Italian is generally spoken . . . We bought some fruit, peaches and pears, and some wooden sabots as characteristic of the native "chassure."

. . . When the Milan diligence arrived, our diligence left Bellinoza and we started for St Gothard . . . Between Faido and Airolo we passed a dreadful gorge, a narrow defile between two perpendicular rocks where there is only room for the road and a wild roaring torrent. It seemed very wonderful that the road could have been made in such a place. It was terrible to look down the precipice which overhung the rushing stream. At Airolo we got something to eat, and then ascended the 28 zigzags of the Italian side of the St Gothard Pass in the dark . . . We arrived at the hotel on the top or "col" of the pass at midnight. The air was bitterly cold and we were very glad to retire to warm bedrooms and comfortable beds.

July 25
In the cold region where we were, there are only 4 houses and 25 people. The hotel, though small, is very comfortable. The hospice, close to the hotel, still continues to receive four travellers and administers to the comfort of many hundreds during the year. Guides and 4 St Bernard dogs are kept at the hotel.

After breakfast we took a guide and ascended Mont Prosa, which is a peak close to the hotel and some 2,000 ft. above the "col" of the pass. Botanizing "en chemin" impeded our progress considerably, so that it was a long time before we reached the summit. And when we did get there, a snowstorm came on and as it drove down quickly with a strong wind, the snow almost froze one side of our faces, and we were obliged to take shelter under a large rock. There we fortified ourselves with food and drink, and the storm not abating we continued the descent and arrived soon white and wet at a stone hovel raised for the purpose of sheltering shepherds and travellers. Here the guide found some wood scattered about the floor and when he had put it together, he produced some matches, and we were soon comfortably seated round a blazing fire. When our clothes were partially dried, the storm being over we set out again and soon gained the banks of the Ticino, which is here quite a small stream. We had seen its source, or one of its sources, when at the top of the mountain . . . We followed the banks of the Ticino . . . and after some delay . . . we gained the coach road, and soon after, our hotel. After tea while we were arranging our plants and writing, two young Germans came in, in a state of great agitation, saying that they had lost a companion coming up the pass from Airolo. A guide and dogs were immediately sent out, and after a short time they returned with the lost man, who did not look much the worse for his adventure. We now determined that Uncle Fraser and I should go on and leave Mr Thompson here. So at 2 am next day

July 26 Wednesday

we two were ready to take the diligence, but alas! it was "completa." We therefore slept till 6 and then started on foot down the Pass for Andermatt. The distance is 8 miles, and the road lies along a bare and rugged valley, without a tree to be seen. This side of the Pass is not so fine as the other, but it is an interesting walk. At times the old road is seen with its large stones, going up and down with the slightest undulations of the ground. At one place we noticed a small iron cross by the side of the road, placed there to mark the spot where some man met with death in the snow . . . (We) soon arrived at Andermatt. Here we took a return carriage to Fluelen. Travelled as quickly as the diligence and more comfortably than diligence travellers . . . After passing through Amsteg and other villages, we arrived in Fluelen as soon as the diligence . . . We embarked immediately on board a steamer on the Lake of Lucerne for Vitznau . . . there we had to wait an hour or two for the train up the Righi. So we took a stroll along the shores of the lake and bathed our feet. At 7 pm we started up the Righi by train. The railway had only been open a month, and it seemed rather foolhardy to risk oneself in it. The ascent is very steep, there are no zigzags but the railway goes round the mountain. The engine pushes the carriage from behind and is not fastened to it. The means of propulsion is by a vertical cog-wheel working on cogs between the lines. It was very dreadful to look down the precipices we passed, and it seemed as if the slightest thing would send us all rolling to the bottom of the mountain. About half way up we passed through a tunnel and over a light iron bridge which spanned a small gorge. There are 3 hotels on the Righi all large ones, and when the train had taken us two-thirds of the way up we had a short walk to our hotel, which was the middle one. Here we found about 200 persons dining; we joined them and then went to bed.

July 27
Rose soon after 5. There was a very strong wind blowing and it seemed wonderful how the hotels could stand there on the top of the hill in all weathers . . . Had a beautiful view although it was not very clear . . . Descended by the railway. The guard has a perfect control over the carriage, stopping it with half a turn of the break (sic) handle. Arrived at the bottom we started by steamer immediately for Lucerne and arrived there in rather more than an hour . . . We then left by train for Berne . . . We had directed our route through Berne in order that I might get a passport there. So as soon as we arrived, we went to the British consul's offices. But alas! we found that consuls generally only have their offices open about 2 hours a day, viz from 10 to 12, or from 11 to 1, and so on till 3 pm. We were therefore too late, and were obliged to remain in Berne till next day. So we . . . saw the Cathedral, the Bears . . . the Palais Federal . . . and attained a general idea of the town. Stayed at the "Gasthof zum Storchen" . . . Not very good.

July 28
Looked about the town again and made some purchases. Repaired at 11 am to the British consul's, where we obtained a passport without the slightest difficulty. Hastened to the French consul's which closes at 12 am and had our passports visa'ed. For this latter service we paid 10 francs each.

Left Berne about 12 am and . . . reached Dijon at 11 pm. We walked about Dijon for ½ hour and saw the old house of M Perluzon . . . Noticed about a score of Prussian soldiers in the station. There are more than 3,000 in the town. Refreshed ourselves in the renowned Dijon "buffet" and started at 12 pm for Paris, which we reached at 6.30, after a fatiguing journey from Berne of 18 hours.

July 29, 30, 31
We spent Saturday, Sunday and Monday in Paris[14]. Stayed at the "Hotel de Lourdes" a cheap and consequently not very convenient place.

On Saturday we saw the Tuileries, the western part of which is thoroughly gutted, the walls alone remaining . . . Many monuments, fountains and beautifully worked lamp posts were thrown from their pedestals or otherwise injured. I counted 8 shot marks on the inside of the Arc de Triomphe, and 85 on the outside, much disfiguring the sculpture. The Palais d'Industrie had a good deal of glass broken . . . Saw the pedestal of the Colonne de Vendome, and the place where it fell . . . Took an omnibus by the river . . . As we passed through the fortifications, the houses all around us were fearfully battered, and many destroyed . . .

On the Sunday we attended service at the "Oratoire" Rue St Honore. Heard a very good discourse. Before the service a minister addressed, in a kind familiar way, 40 or 50 persons, mostly children. The sermon was preached by M. Dhoubres . . .

On Monday we took an omnibus for 3 half-pence each . . . as far as the Place de la Bastille. The Theatre de la Porte St Martin was the greatest wreck I saw, nothing of it was left but heaps of stones . . . We visited Notre Dame also, and noticed marks of robbery. I then went alone to visit Mr Levy and Feinger and their wives. They seemed very pleased to see me and were very kind . . . At 7 pm we left Paris by the express for London and had a very pleasant passage . . . Arrived in London about 6 am.

August 1 Tuesday

I thought of telegraphing to Mary and Mima to tell them to meet us, as I knew they were returning from school on that day; but not knowing their exact address I abandoned the idea, and it was very well I did so, for about 10 o'clock when starting for Wolverhampton, we met them at Euston. We accordingly had a very pleasant journey together home and found Papa, Mama and Nellie anxiously awaiting our arrival at the station. Thus God preserved us through a month's experience of Swiss travelling. And though manifold dangers beset our path, yet by His mercy we passed through them all unscathed, and returned to the bosoms of our respective families . . .

S T Mander August 3 1871

Ornithological expenses 1871

April	Stuffing a stoat	1s. 6d
May 20th	(ditto) a Peggy White throat	1s. 0d
June 12th...........	(ditto) a Barn Owl	2s. 6d
June 12th...........	(ditto) a Turtle Dove	2s. 0d
November 4th...	(ditto) a Sparrow Hawk	2s. 0d
November 4th...	(ditto) a Corncrake	2s. 0d
December 1st....	shot for Filkin	1s. 4d
December 2nd..	Stuffing a Coot	2s. 0d
TOTAL	....	14s. 4d

Printed Circular

Tettenhall, Nr. Wolverhampton. February 1st. 1872
My Dear Friend,

I write with regret to inform you of the decease of William Mortimer[15] who for some years so faithfully discharged the duties of Sarjeant at the Tettenhall College. He suffered for three months stricture of the oesophagus and died on the night of the 22nd. of January from sheer exhaustion produced by starvation.

I think his illness was blessed to his soul and that he died trusting in the merits of his Saviour.

The family thus bereaved and consisting of a wife and five children is left destitute and unprovided for. A collection has been made at the college for their relief amounting to about £10. It has occurred to me that some of the old students who were acquainted with the honest steady and conscientious character of the Serjeant would be willing for his sake to help his family.

If you feel disposed to afford them any aid in their distress I shall be glad to take charge of any donation you may kindly remit. I am, yours faithfully, S.T. Mander.

Two letters addressed to Samuel Mander

8 Fairfax Road, Hampstead. N.W. February 29th. 1872
Dear Sir,

I am sorry that I missed seeing you today, though more so because the two most likely names with which I could have furnished you do not seemed (sic) to have occurred to Mrs Farrar at the time, though she thought of one of them after you were gone.

The Rev. Nathaniel Jennings M.A. of Hampden House, Avenue Road, NW, is accustomed to receive into his house students attending lectures either at University College or at New College. He is a highly respectable scholarly man and I can most cordially recommend him. His wife (a kind and ladylike person) is a daughter of the late Rev. Dr. Vaughan.

One of our professors, the Rev. S. Newth M.A. has also more than once taken a student to reside in his house. They have generally however, if not always, been students attending our own classes. At the same time I do not think that Mr Newth would insist upon this if it should be convenient to him to receive a student at present . . .

Mr Jennings' house, I should think is fully a mile distant from University College and Mr Newth's (25 Clifton Road, St. John's Wood. NW) about ½ a mile further . . .

I am dear Sir, with best respects, yours truly, Wm. Farrar.

1 Camden Square, London NW March 2nd. 1872
Dear Sir,

. . . It occurred to us after you left that we ought to have told you that in addition to the room downstairs, the dining room is always available for evening study if anyone prefers it, and whenever there are more than three, we always recommend some of them to come upstairs.

I would also take this opportunity of saying that if any of our arrangements did not quite accord with your views we should be ready to make such alterations as you might require, if we found it practicable to do so . . .

I remain dear Sir, very truly yours, J. Sewell.

Theodore, 19 years

Among several copies of sermons given by Theodore during the next seven years, the earliest, from 1872, has a note written down the side "prepared for children at York St. Mission – given on March 24th" In spring 1872, he became a student at London University.

79 Denbigh Street, Pimlico. London April 2nd, 1872 10.10 pm.
My very dear Father,

Thank you for your epistle just to hand. I am settling down in my new abode and sphere of operations. Went to Oxford St. this morning. Professor V. very agreeable, good natured man. Set to work. Bought set of apparatus which was ready for me packed in a box, £3. Prof. V's book I bought in Old Burlington St. 10/6. Commenced work. All work on their own book going to Prof. V. or assistant for advice and directions.

Pleasant students, took an interest in my "debut." Young man next me analysing the urine of a person who had diabetes and found it contained 3% of sugar. Dinner at Pamphilon's near Oxford St. and Regent Circus. Boiled mutton, cauliflower, potato, and rhubarb tart and bread 1/4d. Agreeable landlady. Visit this morning from Mr Waterhouse very pleasant. Up this morning at 6.50. Rheumatic pains.

Wednesday morning 8.55

Bacon and kidney for breakfast. Rev. S. Martin and wife out of town till Thursday. Six pictures in sitting room and one in bedroom, very pretty.

Photographs of "Good Shepherd"

"Christ Knocking at the Door."

Three stag scenes, a dog and a squirrel scene, neat oak frames.

Fine drizzling rain coming down. Just going to see Mr Waterhouse and then to Oxford St.

Please thank Mama for her letter and say that in addressing me, she can put Mrs Willimott's name or not first, which she prefers. Mrs Willimott is going to have two or three deal shelves put up for my books with fringe, I don't know whether at her own expense or yours.

With love to all, your most affectionate son, Theodore.

79 Denbigh Street, Pimlico. May 19th, 1872
My very dear Father,

I have just returned from evening service, . . . This afternoon I . . . attended a prayer meeting at Spurgeon's, one of the special ones being held. I enjoyed it immensely: it was so thorough, so earnest, so spiritual. I think no service could be more divested of ceremony . . .

Thank you very much for the list of meetings. I shall try to join them in spirit though I fear I shall not be able to be present in person at any more of them. Every Christian on earth should join to swell the column of the incense of prayer which will rise to Heaven this week. How can a blessing fail to come? "I *will* pour forth my spirit on all flesh" . . . I intend going to Windsor tomorrow for a few hours to get a glimpse and smell of the country as we have a holiday, it being Whit Monday . . .

My best love to all . . . Your very affectionate son, S.T. Mander.

Rhyl May 20, 1872
My dear Theodore,

We have just returned from Caernarvon, Nelly and Lottie and Martin, Miss B., Martha and I, and tomorrow, D.V., I plunge into the depths of the Welsh interior in search of health for mind and body.

I left your dear Mama with only Howard and Margaret and the painters etc. to visit your sisters and see brother Martin, all are well, Martin *very* lively, he is now squealing away as he is preparing for bed. I hope your Mama will run up to town while I am away and see you and take Howard with her.

In your readings, hearings and conversation you will meet with those who apply to the word of God what is called "The Higher Criticism[16]" the object of which, whether applied to sacred or profane history, always is to resolve all that is extraordinary into legend or to accommodate for it in some natural way, it is a method most common now . . . I counsel you most earnestly to give no heed to it . . . It robs Man of his Bible and makes him an orphan in a wilderness on a dark night . . .

Diary of holiday spent with Uncle Fraser and Mr Lees F.L.S. in Switzerland and Italy during July 1872.

Left Wolverhampton July 2 Tuesday . . . arrived in Newhaven to catch the boat for Dieppe at 11.45 pm. Pretty calm passage, but was myself nevertheless very squeamish towards the end, although I took the precaution of lying down the whole time . . .

They travelled via Dieppe, Paris and Lausanne and arrived in Sion on Thursday July 4th.

. . . Glad of the opportunity, we quickly retired to bed, after almost incessant travelling for 72 hours . . . the town of Sion is remarkably situated at the base of the hills, and from this circumstance it doubtless derives its name. One of the said hills is crowned by a church and a seminary for priests, part of the former being so old as the 5th. century; the other hill was formerly fortified by a castle, but now ruins only remain.

Early in the afternoon we proceeded to Sierre, the terminus of the railway, and there took a carriage for Visp a distance of 18 miles . . .

On Saturday morning at 7 o'clock, Uncle Fraser and I set off to walk up the valley of the Visp . . . It was very curious to notice the situations in which the Swiss place their "chalets." We noticed them dotted over the surface of the mountains up to very great heights, and sometimes placed upon apparently inaccessible cliffs. Advantage seemed to be taken of every possible piece of ground where a crop of hay might be obtained or pasturage found for cattle . . . We found the rest of the next day which was Sunday to be very enjoyable, after a weeks hard travelling. Heard a good sermon in the morning from a Low-Church clergyman, who conducted the service assisted by a High-Church man. The contrast between the two was great; the one apparently an outspoken plain country parson, going in years; the other perhaps a highly polished Oxonian, still young and with the "polite" twang of high church reading on his lips.

Monday July 8
Made an excursion to the Schwarz Lee and the Hornli . . . We made meteorological observations in two places and found water to boil at the lake at about 200° F and at the top of the Hornli at about 195° F. Had a very good botanical day, I made a list of about 112 plants without counting the very common ones. Having started at 7 am we returned by 8.30 pm though the distance might have been done in much less time if we had not been botanizing. Our guide, by name Stephan Biner, was acquainted with both the names of plants and the localities in which they grew, and was therefore of great use to us. He was a good type of Swiss mountaineer, being short, brown and wiry, could carry considerable weights with ease for hours together, and can bear any amount of walking and fatigue . . .

Tuesday July 9
. . . Paid a visit to Biner in afternoon, looked over his rare plants; Uncle Fraser bought 70 of them and I invested in a few of his minerals.

Wednesday July 10
. . . to the west lies the great Matterhorn raising its lofty summit with almost perpendicular sides, to a height of 14,700 ft . . . especially sublime did it appear as I saw it at about 4 o'clock one clear morning, standing out cold and still against the blue sky . . . It was from the summit of this Matterhorn that Lord Douglas with two friends and two guides fell in 1865.[17] Their bodies were afterwards found in the snow, at a depth of 4,000 ft from where they fell . . .

Monday July 15
This was the most interesting day we have yet spent for Uncle Fraser and myself. Intending to go to Macugnaga by the New Weiss Thor, we were up at 1 am, but

on looking out of the window the mountains were found to be obscured by a thick mist. And presently up came Napoleon the "porter" to say that the guides (of whom there was a large assemblage that night) thought the weather unfavourable, and said we had better sleep another hour in hopes that it would improve. However in the course of 1 hr. or 1½ hr. the mist did clear off the mountains though the valley of the Visp was still filled with it. The guides then sent word round to the "voyageurs" to say that they thought the weather would now allow of starting. So up we rose at once, dressed, and were down in a few minutes to partake of "café au lait" bread and honey. And at 3.15 we left the hotel while it was still dark, and marched in solemn procession, single file. The cavalcade consisted of a gentleman experienced in Alpine climbing . . . his guides, our two selves and our guide Stephan Biner. After proceeding over the higher parts of the Riffelberg, we walked for about 1 hr. along a very narrow path on a very steep slope overlooking the Gorner Glacier two or three hundred feet below . . .

6 o' clock, arrived at a rock at the side of the glacier where we rested for half an hour and partook of our provisions, which consisted, for the six of us, of 6 bottles of red wine, 1 bottle of tea, (for a journey tea should have no milk and little sugar) 2 large loaves, cheese, 10 eggs, and 1 box of sardines. We found that the guide had also brought with him some prunes and sweet lozenges to aid breathing.

At 6.30 we started again, and kept up a steady pace (four of us being roped together) for 1½ hours . . . At 8 we came across a chamois track, and there we sat down on ropes or alpenstocks and refreshed ourselves . . .

Started again at 8.15 and made for the Cima di Jazzi . . . Reached the top of the Cima at 9.40. The ascent of this mountain we found rather troublesome as it was like walking up the roof of a house covered with hard snow, and had we slipped, we should probably have slid down and perhaps fallen into a crevasse of the glacier. Our march from 6.30 till 9.40 was over one of the largest snowfields in the Alps . . . The snow was probably 5 or 6 feet deep . . . At the summit we obtained a most extraordinary view. The Cima . . . descends on its Italian side in a sheer precipice 6,000 ft in depth and forms a part of the great Monte Rosa precipice, which for depth, breadth and steepness is unequalled in the Alps and perhaps in the world. Standing within five or six feet of the edge I beheld nothing but a vast chasm apparently filled with clouds . . . Here Uncle F wanted to repeat his experiment of boiling water, but unfortunately the spirit in his lamp had evaporated, so we at once descended the steep snow slope on the north side of the mountain, and crossed a depression in the ridge of the precipice . . . when suddenly the appearance of our route underwent a complete change. Instead of toiling over immense fields of snow, we found ourselves, on clambering up a few rocks, on the edge or rather on the side of a fearful precipice . . . The valley 5,000 or 6,000 ft below was obscured by clouds, and when a rent occurred we could see the valley of Macugnaga far away below us. In a nook of the rock we sat down to rest . . . for half an hour till 11 at a height of 11,800 ft. Then the porters resumed their loads and we were roped together . . . We now descended very slowly, making zigzags along the precipitous face of the rocks, sometimes being let down by the rope, sometimes clinging onto a crag with our hands, and sometimes carefully descending steps cut in the ice which lay in the hollows of the rock.

The porters were very agile and appeared wonderfully careless of danger; although carrying heavy loads they rendered us most efficient help. Having descended for some time on the rocks, we reached a steep slope of snow, down which we walked sinking nearly to our knees at each step. At the lower end of this slope we rested again from about 12.40 to 1 . . . We had by this time passed below the clouds, and could see Macugnaga and other villages still thousands of feet below . . . we descended alternate rocks and snow slopes some of which were favourable for a glissade, and at length gained more gradual slopes covered with a scanty vegetation. Crossed one or two avalanches and over a snow bridge which spanned a gorge down which was rushing a wild torrent . . . and at last reached the valley, rather more than 5,000 ft above the sea. Walking . . . through fields of grass and corn we at length reached the Monte Rosa Hotel, Macugnaga, at 5.15 pm having been 14 hours on the road.

This long walk had quite exhausted me, so I took a cup of tea and went to bed at 8.30. We paid our guide 30 francs, and our porters 15 francs and a "bonne main' of 1 franc each.

Friday July 19
Today Uncle F and I left Messrs. Lees and Thompson, and proceeded . . . towards Domo d'Ossola. The valley descends rapidly, and the fir-trees and hay fields of Macugnaga are soon replaced by pretty lanes and cornfields, potato gardens and vineyards, ash trees and Spanish chestnuts, maize and hemp. The German population too of the western part of the valley soon ceases, and dark Italians take their place.

We walked from Macugnaga to Cappomorella, our baggage forming two heavy loads for a man and a woman. The women here are very strong and act as porters almost more frequently than the men, who according to Professor Forbes, leave their valley to gain a livelihood as pedlars and colporteurs.

Took a carriage from Cappomorella to Domo d'Ossola, a very hot and dusty ride . . . There seems a great tendency here to make very long, straight roads, which, though they may increase the rapidity of communication, destroy the charm of travelling. We travelled along one which must have continued 3 miles without the slightest turn. Having left Macugnaga at 9 am and passed Cappomorella at 11.45, staying there till 12.30, we arrived in Domo d'Ossola at 4.15. Dined at the Hotel de la Ville . . . Started by the diligence at 7 for the

Simplon Pass. Unfortunately passed all the beetling cliffs and yawning chasms of this celebrated pass in the dark. But, notwithstanding this misfortune we were able to perceive . . . that this pass must present some very fine scenes of rugged grandeur and of dreary wastes.

Saturday July 20
. . . 5 hours of railway travelling brought us to Bouveret, a station on the south coast of the lake of Geneva. Here we took the steamer and sailed the whole length of sunny Lake Leman . . . Met on board a pleasant young American who had travelled in Italy, Norway and other places, and had lived some time in Germany; also a drunken Swiss who entertained the passengers by an exciting or, more properly, a raving narration of his feelings of hatred and intentions of revenge towards Prussia.

Having Cook's coupons we stayed in Geneva at the large and fashionable Hotel de la Metropole.

Thursday July 24
. . . arrived in Paris about midday. Drove across to the Gare de Saint Lazaire. Rambled through the Champs Elysees. Tuileries still in their ruined state; Colonne Vendome not yet re-erected, Colonne de Juillet in course of reparation.

Saturday July 26
. . . Reached Wolverhampton about 7 pm.

On the whole we enjoyed our tour very well. But on account of the excessive heat and of our not having suitable clothing, the latter part of the journey we found fatiguing and less enjoyable.

Never was I more thankful to reach home, and I render most heartfelt thanks to God for His continued care over us. He attended us through many difficulties and dangers and brought us safely home at last.

Account from a notebook full of reports on sermons attended during 1872/73

Rev. Samuel Martin, Westminster Chapel. April, June, October, December 1872

Westminster Chapel is a large and elegant building, seating about 3,000 persons. It contains two galleries similar to Spurgeon's Tabernacle, and has a very fair organ. The preacher stands upon a semi-circular platform, containing chairs and a reading desk.

The Rev. S. Martin, who has laboured here for the last 30 years, is a man of eminent piety, and of a very kind and generous nature, which at once captivates the heart of all who enjoy a private interview with him. I do not consider Mr Martin a man of great intellectual power, though for his other excellent qualities he fairly claims a place among the "principes" of the Nonconformist body of ministers, as also for the great work he has been made the instrument of accomplishing. The chief feature of his character which I have mentioned, appears prominently in the performance of his ministerial duties. His sermons are almost all addressed to the converted; he enjoys feeding them gently with the soft milk of the Word, comforting and encouraging, as a shepherd his lambs. In my opinion Mr Martin does not do sufficient to rouse his flock to more strenuous efforts in the Lord's service, to real practical work and constant self-abnegation for the sake of the dying multitudes around; and certainly he does not excel in proclaiming the thunders of Sinai, and the reality of future punishment, to dead or dreaming souls, or to those living in open sin.

Mr Martin has many institutions connected with his Church, among which I may mention 4 Sunday Schools, a Shoe-Black Institution, and an Orphanage for girls.

Lapworth Rectory Birmingham August 26 1872
Dear Sir,

In reply to your note received this morning I am happy to say the name of Mander has long been well known and respected in this parish – being now represented by Mr Robert Mander of Ireland's Farm, my worthy parishioner.

I shall be happy, if you so instruct me, to search the Register for any entries of this name prior to 1700. The charge is 3/6 for each entry, should you wish a certificate of each entry. I should not think there can be many entries prior to 1700. I have myself noticed the name of the family to go back about 200 years.

If I can do so between now and post-time I will try and ascertain the earliest entry in the name of Mander.

I am, yours faithfully, John R.T. Eaton.

After a close search I find ten entries up to the year 1703 inclusive. The earliest is Thomas son of Samuel Mander Buried September 16 1675.

The Vicarage, Aston Cantlow, Henley-in-Arden August 27 1872
Dear Sir,

Our parish registers date from the year 1560. I have searched from the year 1700 back to 1672, and find the name Mander, more frequently Maunder, occurring 7 times.

Were I to send you a certificate of these 7 entries, my fee would be 2/7 for each, including stamp.

If you wish it I can search back to as far as 1560, and should I find any more entries the same charge would be made for certificates, and I leave it to you to send what you think well for searches, suggesting that the legal charge would be 6d. for every year.

I am, yours truly, T.F. Fagge.

A notebook started in the summer of 1872, begins with reports on visits made to various factories

Fred Walton and Co. Japanners and Hardware Manufacturers August 27 '72
Trays – Papier mâché.
12 to 36 layers of paper pasted together on a block. Edges torn to prevent creases. Dried in hot room.

Saturated with hot linseed oil to harden. When dried in oven can be worked like wood. Japanned about 12 times, each coat being dried and rubbed with pumice-stone.

Ornamentation

Gold leaf laid onto with water. Pattern painted over gold with "asphaltum." Uncovered gold taken off with wet rag. Asphaltum removed by turpentine. Other painting added by hand. Handed up with "rotten-stone."

Elkington and Co. Manufactory of Plated Silver Goods August 30 '72
Plating
Articles to be silvered or gilded are hung by copper wires on copper rods arranged in parallel rows over vats containing cyanide of silver or gold; one end of each copper rod rests on a copper bar running the whole length of a vat, and which is in connection with a battery. The solutions are replenished with metal, by plates of it hung in the liquid. Parts of vessels not to be plated are coated with a blue varnish before being immersed in the metallic solutions.

Saw a vessel gilded inside in about ½ minute, after being dipped in an acid to make it perfectly clean.

Vessels pass through two solutions in the course of plating; the first leaves them dull, the second bright.

Visited Elkington's extensive shew-rooms.

Gillott and Sons Steel Pen Manufactory August 30 '72
Pens
Steel rolled in long strips.

Large rooms in which hundreds of girls are at work, each having a small punching or other machine worked by hand, the die being raised and lowered by means of a perpendicular screw.

Some dies only cut out the exterior of the pen; others at the same time stamped the makers name. Others formed the two side slits and others again slit the pen at the end.

The last process in the formation of the pens is the bending of them into their semi-cylindrical shape. This is done by similar machines to those already described . . .

One great reason for the large amount of money made by Gillott, is the fact that females are almost exclusively employed in his works.

Above 150 million pens are made here annually.

Hartley, Thorneycroft and Co. Iron Works August 31 '72 . . .
This firm casts its own rolls etc. and makes all its own machinery, besides mining a good deal of its own coal . . .

1500 men employed, in two sets, working 10 hours each.

Fires allowed to go out about midday Saturday. Bricklayers etc. come to work at 12 on Sunday night to repair furnaces in order that the fires may be lighted at midday on Monday.

The Vicarage, Aston Cantlow, Henley-in-Arden August 30 1872
Dear Sir,

I have carefully searched the registers of this parish from 1700 back to 1560. The earliest entries of the Maunders is in 1639. "Henicus, filuus Henrice Maunder' I do not think I have passed over any but I may have done so among the very early entries, for they are all written in old English characters, some are very badly written, and some are become very indistinct by reason of their antiquity. The Certificates I send are of:-

Weddings.......2 Burials.......10 Baptisms.......16 = 28

Fees (Certificates).......£3.10 Stamps.......4s.4 = £3.12.4

Not knowing your means I hesitate to make the legal charge for searchings. I leave it with you; simply saying that if you are well to do in the world and are disposed to gauge your liberality by your means (excuse my plain speaking) your offering will be most acceptable, as I have a family of 17 children, and the Income of the living of Aston Cantlow barely exceeds £80. Let me add that for legal purposes, I will gladly repeat my search.

I am, yours truly, T.F. Fagge.

Anno Dom 1675
Thomas ye sonne of Samuel Maunder, buried September 16

1676
John the sonne of Samuel Maunder and his wife was baptised March 16

1679
Samuel the son of Robert Maunder was baptised January 4

1683
Anne the daughter of Robert Maunder and his wife was baptised April 22
An the daughter of Robert Maundre was buried October 20 1688
Robert the son of Robert Maunder was buried October ye 28th

1696

Mary ye daughter of Henry Maunder bapt. June 1st buried June 20th.

1700

John ye son of Samuel Mander bury'd January 28th.

1701

Samuel Mander jun'r bury'd August 21st.

1703

Matthew the son of William Mander and Martha James bapt. October 27

I, John Richard Turner Eaton, Rector of the Parish of Lapworth in the county of Warwick, do declare that the above are true copies of the several Entries in the Register Book of the Parish aforesaid.

John R.T. Eaton Rector of Lapworth 3 September 1872

79 Denbigh Street, Pimlico October 17 1872

My Dear Father,

. . . I hope you and Mama have enjoyed your stay in Nottingham and are both all the better for it . . . I take in the Daily News and try to get half an hour to read it before I start to Kensington in the morning which I do at 9.30. I enjoy the reading of it very much. The papers are so cheap now and contain so much valuable and interesting information that I think it forms an important part of ones education to read them.

I attended a junior and senior German class at University College last night to see which would (suit) me best. Neither are very advanced and I shall accordingly join the senior one. This will be the best method for me to continue my German studies. There only a few in the class and I shall enjoy learning with a class better than working alone. Fee £2.12.6 for the session or £1.1 per term. I suppose I had better pay for the session . . . Mr Val asked me for my fee today, viz £12 for the term. Can I have it please soon. He is collecting them at once; a wise plan I think for one of the students . . . last session went off without paying at all.

Now with much love to all, I remain ever, your affectionate son,

S.T. Mander.

P.S. I am sorry to want money so soon. But I have only about £6 left. It has all been properly spent. S.T.M.

Royal Mint Visited October 28 1872

Gold received in ingots. Saw bars of gold averaging £700 each in value . . . Sovereigns weighed by self-acting balances costing 250 guineas each. A pile of coin placed above, sovereigns drop in the balance-pan one by one, and according to the position in which they place the balance, fall into a short-weight, just-weight or over weight box. Sovereigns of wrong weight remelted . . .

Tower of London Visited October 28 1872
This noble edifice, round whose hoary head gather more numerous reminiscences of historic interest than are connected with any other building in England, still stands in all its gloomy grandeur on the banks of old Father Thames . . . from the first successful establishment of our national liberties in Magna Charta, unto the present day of free and enlightened thought, and of rapid and steady reform, the Old Tower of London has stood gravely looking on in silence, increasing gradually in size, and receiving within its walls the frequent victims of royal caprice or popular indignation. And, during the swift flight of time, all the old surroundings of the building have changed. The merry whistling of birds, and sweet odours of flowers borne on that breeze from neighbouring fields and woods have disappeared . . . These things are all swept away by the ever increasing tide of trade . . . Instead of the cheerful chirp of the bird is to be heard the fierce shriek of the steam-engine, instead of the wreaths of smoke that formerly rose on the pure air, volumes of steam pour from the fiery throat of the locomotive, on every side "manufacture taints the ambient air." Instead of the sweet odour of flowers, the atmosphere is filled with foul and unwholesome smells, pestilent vapours, rising from the fish stalls of Billingsgate . . . and the entangled shipping of St. Katherine's Dock . . .

Bank of England Visited with Uncle and Aunt Harper December 18 1872
Bank Parlour
Large and lofty room presenting an air of great comfort, thick carpet, 3 fires, oil lamps, no gas. Also a small and equally comfortable committee room, at the end of the Bank Parlour. In the large room the rise and fall of interest is decided, and thence telegraphed to all parts of the world. Thousands throughout the world weekly await the decision of this Council with breathless anxiety.

Printing Rooms
Here bank-notes of all values and for every part of the British Empire are printed. The ordinary announcement of "Pay the bearer' etc. is printed in one room, and the notes are then passed through another room, where they receive vitality, ie. they are stamped with a number, date and signature of the Chief Cashier. Ingenious arrangement for altering the number between each note . . .

A picket of soldiers is lodged in the Bank every night. They are allowed as much beer and cheese as they can devour, and their officer receives £1 per night for his dinner.

Rev. J.J. Gregory, Park Chapel, January 19 1873
The Chapel is an old but poor building, devoid of all architectural beauty, but seating I should think from 1,000 to 1,500 people. This complement is constantly obtained by the present clergyman, Rev. J.J. Gregory, in fact the church is frequently filled and crowded to excess. Mr Gregory is an Evangelical, belonging to the lowest of the Low[18]. His earnestness is extreme, and his love for souls attracts the attention of large numbers, who with many a clergyman would remain indifferent, and almost oblivious of the parson's presence in his parish . . .

Rev. Simpson, St Clement Danes, Strand January 26 Morning
This is one of the old London churches, standing in one of the busiest thoroughfares and obtaining a better congregation than the City Churches. The building is of that white stone which constitutes the material of so many London Churches. The interior is fitted with oak pews of the antique fashion . . . A portion of the roof is elegantly decorated with the rose and thistle worked in plaster. The chancel contains a very beautiful triple window . . .

. . . The curate did not read the lesson etc. in the usual sing-song manner, his accents were modulated in a very curious manner, and the performance of his lectional devotions, frequently approached a serio-comic style.

In accordance with an ancient and venerable custom, the names of six individuals were published as wishing to enter into the bonds of "holy matrimony" and the congregation called upon to declare any objection they might have to that honorable proceeding.

The sermon was preached by a strange clergyman, and was a model of composition; moreover it contained clear and ample Gospel truth, but was delivered in such a manner as to lead the congregation to believe that the clergyman was just performing a duty imposed on him by God and that all they had to do, was to listen and go their way.

Pimlico January 27 1873
My very dear Father,

I met Mary, Mima and Nellie on Friday as arranged and took them to Clapham. They seemed rather home-sick, especially Nellie who was filled with gloomy foreboding concerning the reception she would receive from Mrs Gill. However they were the first arrivals at school and had a pleasant chat in the drawing room, before I left, with Mrs Gill who was as usual very merry and kind and delighted to see them, especially Mary . . . I heard an excellent sermon last night (in the) Surrey Chapel from the Rev. Newman Hall. He took for his text "and they all slumbered and slept and at midnight there was a cry made." He applied the words very appropriately to the late catastrophe at Dungeness. In the course of his remarks he happened to touch on the Temperence question, saying that very likely the crew of the vessel which ran into the "Northfleet" were intoxicated and he thought that the proportion of casualties caused at sea by drunkenness must reach one-third of all that occur. He told us moreover that he had had the "privilege" of being an abstainer for 30 years, remarking that intemperance is an evil which every philanthropist, every patriot and every Christian ought to seek by all means in his power to diminish and destroy. Mr Hall said that he had heard the other day in conversation, of a law that has recently passed the French Legislature to the effect that every person found inebriated should be fined 5 francs and the fine increased at each repetition of the offence up to 500 francs . . . Got on pretty well at dancing party, Blackheath. Was the only gent. except Mr Smith senior who did not dance. One looks very foolish standing about talking for five or six hours when all the rest are dancing. I therefore left early with another gentleman who was returning to town by the last train.

. . . Very much love to yourself, dear Mama, Lottie and Martin. Ever your very affectionate son, S. Theo. Mander

Sermon reports

Rev. Dr. Stoughton, Kensington Chapel February 9 Morning
Chapel a plain unadorned building of moderate size and classic architecture. Good organ and well conducted singing. Exhibits strikingly the principle of Dissenters of eschewing all attempts to attract and all possibilities of deception, by a display of architectural decoration or other mere outward form, which might gratify the eye and veil the heart . . .

Rev. J.G. Rogers, Grafton Chapel February 9 Evening
Moderate sized building. External appearance neat and graceful, being in Gothic style. Interior comfortably fitted up with oak pews. Very respectable congregation. Good organ and singing.

Sermon 1 John II.17 [19] – relating to the different ambitions and various fame of the five illustrious personages who died during last month, viz:- Napoleon 111, Lord Bulwer Lytton, Sir Stephen Lushington, Professor Sedgwick and Rev. Baptist Noel.

Report of a visit to the Foundling Hospital[20]

February 16 1873
Large but gloomy chapel, lighted with gas by day. Very numerous congregation. Chief interest, of course, centred in the band of 200 to 300 young children, boys

and girls, who occupied the galleries on each side of the organ, and sang the psalms, responses etc. It is indeed a most pleasing sight, and one which cannot fail to call forth the admiration and generosity of all visitors, to behold this goodly array of little girls and boys, gathered in their earliest hours from abodes of filth and misery, and received into this institution where they are fed healthily, clothed warmly, educated intelligently, and trained lovingly in habits of industry and piety.

The service was somewhat longer than that usually adopted in churches, and was rendered specially impressive by the joyful singing of so many innocent voices.

After service, visitors were admitted to the dining rooms, where the children, after marching in in orderly procession, and having joined in the prayer of gratitude for temporal mercies offered up by one girl standing in the centre of the hall, sat down to a hearty dinner of hot roast beef and potatoes. The boys and girls dine in separate apartments, except some few of very tender age, who partake at the same table of more delicate fare than their older companions, viz of minced meat and mashed potatoes.

Behind the building is an extensive play-ground, where seats are scattered on grassy lawns under the shade of numerous trees. I also saw the boys' school-room and a room devoted to the memory of former benefactors of the Institution. Here are autographs of monarchs, statesmen and men of literary fame, who have from time to time interested themselves in the poor forsaken Foundlings. I noticed the names of Albert, Dickens etc. etc. Here also are preserved tokens deposited by the parents on the admission of their children, in order to their recognition if necessary; they consist of brooches, necklaces, coins, nails, pins, wire etc. etc. I noticed this text on a wall; "When my father and mother forsake me, then the Lord will take me up."

Sermon reports

Rev. Machonokie, St Alban the Martyr. February 23 1873

. . . I confess that in visiting this place of worship, I was impelled rather by curiosity than by hope of profit. I watched the service with great interest, since it has such high repute for advanced ritualistic observances.

I arrived at 11 o'clock; the morning service had just terminated and the service of Holy Communion, the most imposing of the day, was commencing. On entering, I found that it was thought necessary to reverse the order of Nature, and separate the men and women. Having sat down, I looked in the direction where the officiating curate is usually to be seen; but what was my surprise when I beheld three priestly individuals, arrayed in gorgeous vestments, and performing an incomprehensible series of evolutions before an altar which bore on its surface several candles. Several vestured acolytes, standing or kneeling as circumstances demanded, on the steps of the altar, attended to the various wants of the priests. Above, seven holy lamps hung in mid-air burning their "everlasting oil," and shedding the sweet odour of incense around. The meaningless ceremonies of bowing and genuflection, diversified occasionally by the repetition of prayers or psalms according to a system of unnatural and ridiculous intonation, continued for about the space of three-quarters of an hour, when the gaily attired officials retired in solemn procession, after resuming their square priestly caps. The Rev. Machonokie now ascended the pulpit, clothed in a white surplice, over which hung a short black cape and a scarlet hood; there were likewise two purple bands hanging from his shoulders and bearing on them various emblematic devices. He took for his text Luke XVIII.37 "And they told him that Jesus of Nazareth passeth by."

The sermon contained the leaven of the gospel, but was devoid of all vigour and intellectual power; I considered the references to Lent, and advice concerning its observation, weak and superstitious.

This good remark was made:- "Blind Bartimeus could not see Jesus although He passed close to him; we cannot see or perceive God although we dwell in the midst of Him."

After sermon, another series of mockeries was observed, and then the Holy Communion was administered to two or three persons. The blessing of the bread and wine was attended with similar foolish ceremonial observances to those I have frequently seen in French Catholic churches.

After careful examination, I could detect but little difference between this High Church Ritual and a bona fide Roman Catholic service. And although I tried to be charitable, I came away utterly disgusted. To think that the holy, and humanizing religion of our blessed Lord, intended to comfort, guide and enlighten us while travelling through this lower world, should be converted into such a series of degrading mummeries! We see in this Ritualistic movement, one of the most subtle and crafty plots of Satan, by which he would drag us down from the eminence on which we enjoy the light of God's gospel, and would plunge us again into the darkness of the middle ages . . .

St James' Hall, Rev. Newman Hall. February 23 1873 3 pm.
A striking contrast to the service I witnessed this morning. A large hall crowded with persons of every sect and denomination. The Litany read in a suitable intelligent manner. Several hymns were sung, everybody being able to join, as a copy was placed in every hand on entering. A simple vigorous, earnest sermon, from the text, "And shall not God avenge His own elect?" Luke XVIII.7.

It was very refreshing to be able to join with a large body of people intelligibly and unitedly singing the praises of Almighty God, after the empty mockery of religion I saw at St Albans' into which no one could sincerely and heartily enter.

The family at Glen Bank. Meteorological equipment including a rain gauge can be seen on the far right.

Glen Bank, Tettenhall Wolverhampton. February 24 1873

My very dear Theo,

In looking back twenty years I well remember that the snow lay on the ground about as it does now, perhaps a little deeper, and I thought how well off I was in my comfortable bedroom at St Paul's Terrace with my dear little baby, then the only one, and for whom your Papa and I had asked our Father in Heaven, to whom we at once devoted our little son. I would fain believe that God accepted the gift and will ever use you as His own and keep you unspotted from the world.

May you (if it be His will) have many happy returns of the anniversary of your birthday and I certainly hope tomorrow will be a peaceful and joyous day to you . . .

Now with much love believe me dear Theodore, your very affectionate Mother.

Glen Bank, Tettenhall February 24 1873

My dear Theodore,

It is with much gratitude and satisfaction I take pen in hand to give you a birthday greeting . . .

It is but your due that I should tell you how much comfort your dear Mama and I derive from your steady and consistent endeavours after the good and the useful and the true . . . may you have many bright and happy anniversaries of your birthday, each telling of victory and progress and each finding you the centre of a wider circle of good and Godly influence.

. . . I propose coming up the town on Thursday and hope to take tea with you the same evening. We are all well . . . Brothers and sisters all sound, what matter for praise and hopeful onlooking.

Ever your affectionate father, Samuel S. Mander.

Grafton Chapel Missionary Service. March 2 1873
Rev. Macfarlane formerly of Leifn, now of New Guinea, made an earnest and suitable appeal for money, but more especially for the prayers of Christians He described the introduction of the Gospel into New Guinea, also into Leifn and its beneficent effect on the inhabitants of the latter island. How the extensive and disgusting practices of cannibalism, and the system of idolatry which they found, have entirely disappeared . . .

Rev. John Moffat gave an account of the Matabele Mission. The failure of the Makalolo Mission on account of the death of the missionaries, the war-like character of the Matabele and the origin of the tribe; the despotism of its former and present chief, their complete system of "espionage" by which the people are subdued in awe at the supposed omniscience of the chief; the enforced celibacy of the warriors, and consequent licentious immorality of the tribe . . . After many years labour not one convert is known of among the Matabele.

Highbury April 1 1873
My very dear Father,

Many thanks for the money, sorry for not acknowledging before. Last Thursday Tom and I and some of the Baines's spent a very pleasant couple of hours at St James' Hall. There were no instrumentalists and the vocal music was mostly part singing performed by Mr Leslie's renowned and accomplished choir. The programme offered a most choice selection of part-songs, etc. and was highly appreciated and enjoyed by us all.

On Friday I spent a pleasant evening with Mary, Mima, Nellie and Ellen Pearsall at the Misses Devenish's.

Saturday was wholly given up to the Boat Race. Tom and I went down to Chiswick with the Baines' and had a most lively and enjoyable afternoon. The scene on the river and its banks, so well described in the papers was wonderful, the weather perfectly charming and the race most satisfactory to my hopes and expectations. We returned home with the Baines' and spent the evening at their house.

On Sunday I took tea with Mr and Mrs Gill and took M., M. and N. to chapel.

Do you contemplate going to Vienna, Switzerland or both? If the former should not rooms be secured at once; if present price is £1.1s per night what will it be in a few weeks time . . .

Would you please ask Mama to send me a good sized bag by Mander when he comes, for bringing home necessary clothes at Easter. I have here only my large portmanteau . . .

I intend to come home on Thursday week for a week or ten days . . .

Very much love to yourself, dear Mama and all.

Your affectionate son, S. Theo Mander.

Sermon reports

Rev. Stopford Brooke[21], Chapel of Ease to St James', Piccadilly. April 6
John XIV 16

. . . Depth of thought characterized the discourse, as it does the printed sermons by the same author, but Rev. Stop. Brooke's spoken sermons are not so pleasing as his written ones, on account of his disagreeable delivery.

Rev. Canon Liddon, St Paul's Cathedral April 6 '73 3 pm

. . . God works out His plans not only by direct religious teaching, action or influence, but also by many indirect means, making the works of Nature, and science, and art, and civilization and learning generally to subserve His great ends . . .

Rev. Mark Wilkes, Holloway Chapel 1/6/73

Mr Wilkes has a beautiful chapel . . . The roof is supported by clustered Gothic pillars of delicate shaft; the side pews are raised in tiers; there are one or two stained glass windows, and a beautiful organ with bright iron pipes delicately decorated with a blue pattern; above the organ is an illuminated text . . .

Natural History notebook

June 17. Noticed how the distance between myself and persons walking in the neighbourhood, on a quiet evening, was apparently greatly lessened, when the sound of their footsteps entered my ear at right angles.

July 22. The peculiar appearance of clouds before a thunderstorm which is so very characteristic of an electrical state of the atmosphere, may be described as an unusual distinctness of outline strongly contrasting the dark black rain-clouds with the lighter colour of the atmosphere beyond, which is often tinged yellow. The fringed edges and scattered fragments likewise become very distinctly visible.

Llanerch Farm, Llanfairfechan. August 15th, 1873
My very dear Father,

We were very glad to hear from you again this morning. I am sorry to say that your letter did not find Mama in the happiest condition possible. She is suffering from a bad attack of face-ache and has done so for several days. The swelling is very painful and shews no sign of abatement. She went as usual until today but now thinks it advisable to remain in bed. A leech is contemplated.

We are enjoying ourselves immensely, the rest of us. We have ascended several lofty summits, visited waterfalls, boated, bathed and explored almost the whole neighbourhood. The elevated peak of Penmaenmawr (1500 ft.) has felt the pressure of our venturous feet. Aber waterfall has cooled our heated brows. The "fern hollows" and bare table lands have all witnessed our ardour for exploration. Some of us bathe every day and we enjoy the boating very much. This morning I took Howard out a quarter of a mile in a boat and there we anchored and bathed. During half the tide the water is shallow for more than ½ a mile. After bathing five of us had an hours row.

I don't think a detailed description of our domestic interior would interest you much and therefore I won't impose it on you. Suffice it to say that we are *very* comfortable and occupy a sitting room and five bedrooms. I am glad to say we are not annoyed with the usual concomitant horrors of a farmhouse. There are horses and cows, fowls and ducks, but no pestilent yard or stagnant pool emitting noisome effluva or breeding malaria. I have just made a tour of the premises and find nothing worse than a small heap of manure at a distance from the house and emitting a pleasant and healthy odour. The only nuisance to which we are subject is a plague of earwigs, which obstinate and obnoxious little animals persistently invade Martha's bedroom until the threshold is heaped with their dead bodies, metaphorically speaking.

In closing I must say that we are all very happy and doing full justice to the general appetising and energising influences of our position.

With best love from us all to yourself and Mary. Your ever affectionate son
S. Theodore Mander.

Minehead Quay, Somerset. August 28th, 1873
My very dear Father,

. . . Enjoying myself much. We drove from Bridgewater to Minehead on Tuesday, a distance of 27 miles in Mr S's horse and pony traps.

When I say "we" you must understand Mr and Mrs S., Tom and his sister and myself. We are making the above mentioned town (very remote from the world) our headquarters and make excursions thence into the surrounding country.

Our lodgings are within two or three yards of the quay and harbour, which latter is constantly filled with schooners, sloops and fishing smacks. The swell from the Atlantic rolls in on the shore in magnificent grandeur and breaks on the beach with the noise of thunder. We had a very pleasant bathe before breakfast on Wednesday and a row afterwards. Today Tom, Sally and I have had a walk of some 14 miles over the healthy hills and richly wooded combes of Exmoor returning by a bluff cliff overhanging the Channel which was lashed into fury by a stiff S.W. breeze.

. . . Tom and I think of going down by steamer tomorrow, if fine, (for it has rained a good deal) to Ilfracombe . . .

I hope you have enjoyed yourself very much at Llanerch etc. and are all the better for the stay there.

. . . I must now close, with best love to all. Ever your affectionate son
S. Theo Mander.

During the Autumn of 1873, Theodore continued to work as a lay preacher delivering sermons at Bilston Mission Room in October and at York Street in November.

Circular

Glen Bank, Tettenhall, Nr. Wolverhampton December 1st, 1873
Dear Sir,

In the capacity of a former student at Tettenhall College, I write to you on behalf of Herr H. Pomnitz whose name has been so long known in connection with that institution.

Mr Pomnitz has occupied the position of a Master at the College during two periods of three years each. His uniform kindness and good nature combined with an unflagging energy and an untiring attention to his scholastic duties, which he has ever discharged with efficiency, have not failed to secure for him the esteem and respect, it is believed, of all who have studied under him.

In prospect of Marriage, Mr Pomnitz is about to leave the College and intends under the altered circumstances of his life, to return to his native country. A subscription has been set on foot to present him with a Purse at Christmas; and if, as an old pupil of his, you would like to assist in the Gift please remit your Donation to me as early as possible.

It may be as well to state that Mr Pomnitz lost some years ago nearly all the savings of his early life.

I am, yours very truly, S. Theo Mander.

Flora Paint

Diary December 1873

Vere Smith has come today to stay til Monday. Two very pleasant girls, school fellows of Mary and Mima are also staying with us for a few weeks. Flora Paint[22] of Halifax, Canada, very merry girl. Mary Lloyd of St. Ives, Hunts.

December 29th Monday

Took Flora P., Mary L., Mima and Vere Smith to Birmingham to see Society of Arts annual picture exhibition also Town Hall.

December 31st Wednesday

Took a ride with Jenny, Flora P. and Mr Avery. Attended watch night service at night. Combination of four dissenting Chapels. The body of the Chapel full. Reverends Horton, Stewart and Dunbar officiated. Very solemn and enjoyable.

Thus ends a year for the boundless mercies and rich blessings of which be endless praise to God.

1874 – 1879

Anno Domini 1874
January 1st
Am having a few days holiday, very happy, merry family just now. Ourselves complete and supplemented by ecretions (sic) from without, Ellen Pearsall[23], Flora Paint, Mary Lloyd, Michael Parker and Henry, the last two being lads from Blackheath School for Missionary sons. The new year opens with fine weather. Oh may all its experiences be bright and happy. May I be enabled to live a consistent Christian life before our friends and thus exercise a great influence for good . . .

Ornithological record, all the birds being listed by Theodore under their Latin names – common names have been added in brackets followed, where necessary, by their modern classifications

1874 January Glen Bank

1 ...... *Pyrgita domestica*
2 ...... *Erythaca rubecula* (Robin)
3 ...... *Parus caerulcus* (Blue tit)
4 ...... *Parus major* (Great tit)
5 ...... *Corvus frugilegus* (Rook)
6 ...... *Turdus viscivorus* (Mistle thrush)
7 ...... *Turdus musicus* (Thrush – *Turdus philomelos*)
8 ...... *Sternus vulgaris* (Starling)
9 ...... *Merula vulgaris* (Blackbird – *Turdus merula*)
10 ...... *Columba palumbus* (Wood pigeon)
11 ...... *Fringilla coelebs* (Chaffinch)
12 ...... *Accentor modularis* (Hedge sparrow – *Prunella modularis*)

Merridale Crescent (Wolverhampton) February 24th
My dear Theodore,

As I shall not have the pleasure of seeing you tomorrow I feel constrained to send you a line of greeting, not because I think you would miss it or be benefited by it, but because I should not like to seem unmindful of so important a crisis as your "coming of age." And first let me say in true old fashioned form "I wish you many many happy returns of the day."

. . . I would . . . express my earnest desires that God would grant you . . . His richest spiritual gifts, which alone can make your life a truly happy one . . . Believe me with much love, your affectionate cousin Kate . . .

Basford House, Whalley Range. Manchester 24th. February 1874
My dear nephew,

The presence of imperative duties at this moment, prevents my coming to Wolverhampton to aid in the celebration of tomorrow. I am very sorry for this, but I must not allow the important and interesting occasion to pass without offering my sincere congratulations that you have been preserved to arrive at man's estate, and to find yourself surrounded in things both temporal as well as spiritual with so "goodly a heritage." Such privileges entail weighty obligations, and I don't doubt but you will earnestly strive to be found faithful in all things.

My dear daughters, who represent us, carry with them a little present from me which I hope will be found useful.

Believe me, always Faithfully Yours, Henry B Jackson.

To S.T. Mander Esq.
Sir,

We wish to make you a present of a Riding Whip on your coming of age and wish you a long life and a prosperous one. We are Sir, your obedient servants J. Gryce, C. Harris, J. Lees, E. Bason, J. Patrick, M. Tifiton

Glen Bank 25th February 1874

Notebook and diary

February 25. My 21st birthday
A very happy time (not without regret for past misdeeds) The occasion was heartily celebrated by loving friends.

25th. Select dinner party of about 20 at home.

26th. Lunch of perhaps 30 company of juvenile friends, followed by prayer, congratulation meeting in the drawing room.

26th evening A great dinner in the Agricultural Hall. About 200 present, relations, friends, work people from St John's Street, all joined in convivial celebration of the occasion – acting by clerks etc afterwards. After such testimony of good will and affectionate solicitude as I received on this too extensively observed occasion, I ought indeed to do something in life. I must strive, while overflowing with gratitude and love to my Heavenly Father and to my earthly friends, to live a *good*, *useful*, *active* life abounding in deeds of benevolence, kindness and love. Received as presents about 70 books besides other things.

Basford House March 5th 1874
My dear Theodore,

As you see I have made great efforts to fulfil my promise to you in the belief that you will do the same. I think you can hardly fail to like this photograph of Mama, it is generally pronounced excellent. I wish I could say the same for Edie's and mine which are great failures, however you shall have better ones soon I hope. Papa has promised me one of his but I do not know when I shall get it, or you either – but I will not forget. We had our New Year's gathering last night, which had been put off on account of Mr Tippett's illness. We mustered 18 strong, all one family – rather more extensive than yours even. Papa says he can heartily sympathise with John Gilpin "who little thought when he set out of running such a rig." It was very good of you to ask us to your celebration. We enjoyed it immensely as you know. We got too, not only pleasure but a little good – but that I think you will scarcely believe.

With very much love to Uncle, Aunt and the others, Your affectionate cousin, Gertrude F Jackson.

Diary

April 4th Monday
My dear sisters Mary and Mima have started today with Papa and Mama for Wiesbaden where they are to educate, D.V. Emily Dickinson with them. Nellie goes to school again same day, Mrs Gill's.

17 Gracechurch Street, London 23 April 1874
My dear Mr Theodore,

Your letter found me in bed with a little attack of fever and ever since there has been sickness in my house, otherwise it would certainly not have remained so long unanswered.

Will you permit me to tell you with what gratification I have watched your career opening and what great hopes I cherish of your usefulness not only to our business but also to society.

Many men desirous of fulfilling their mission in this world conscientiously, are bewildered because they cannot clearly see where their duty lies. This, fortunately, is not your case. Providence has placed you in the position you hold in connection with the business and expects you to do your duty by it heartily and earnestly, recollecting that the welfare of many persons will depend greatly upon your so doing.

I am looking forward with much pleasure to your advent here and should you come will endeavour to make your stay as agreeable and profitable as possible.

I remain, Yours very faithfully, Henry Clark.[23]

London July 11 1874
My dear Mrs Mander,

No doubt you will be rather surprised to hear from me but circumstances demand it.

Thank you very much for the photograph. I have chosen the one with the two silver birches after a great deal of deep thought. I write to apologise for the untidy appearance of Nellie's letter, and also to contradict her statement of my avarice. I hope you will receive the former and forget the latter.

I think Theodore's photograph is very good indeed, much better than any former one.

Last Sunday evening Mrs Smith and I went to Spurgeon's Tabernacle and heard as usual a simple earnest sermon from its minister.

I have not had any letter from home by this mail and I shall soon be a case of "Alone in London" for Mrs Gill intends to send me off in a fortnight's time. I suppose we shall soon have the pleasure of seeing Theodore – Nellie just manages to restrain her feelings.

Please remember me kindly to all and with kind regards to Mr Mander, Believe me, Yours very affectionately, Flora E Paint.

17 The Cedars Road, Clapham Common, London. Thursday
Dear Mrs Mander,

We saw Mr Theodore on Sunday and we are expecting and anxious to hear from him again tonight as to the probable result of his Examination work.

Tomorrow he and his sister are to have a day of sight-seeing in London. Theodore invited Flora also but this I did not accept.

I have received no letter yet from Mrs John so that it leaves me terribly in the dark as to what to do for Flora.

She seems to have a very fixed impression that she will not return home quite yet, and therefore I think if at all convenient to you I will accept for her your kind invitation for the fortnight . . .

As soon as letters come from Mr Paint I will forward them and write you as to future arrangements.

Excuse this hurried note, do not trouble to write to me – unless you cannot now receive Flora.

How very chaste and elegant your present to our darling Jessie. My heart nearly breaks at the idea of our parting.

Yours very truly, Catherine Gill.

Council of Education, Kensington Museum Royal College of Chemistry,
South Kensington. July 21st 1874
Dear Sir,

In answer to your inquiries I beg to say:-

1 The term begins about the middle of Oct.

2 Apply to:-
Professor Dr. Hofmann[24], Berlin University, Berlin – and you will be sure to get a reply.

3 Terms of Laboratory attendance very moderate, something like £6 per half year.

If your son should decide upon going to Berlin I shall be happy to give him an introduction to some friends of mine who would assist him in getting comfortable lodgings . . . Dr. Hofmann always takes particular interest in English students and I have no doubt your son would greatly profit by a stay of one or two years with that eminent chemist.

I remain, dear sir, Yours very faithfully, Wm. Valentine

Holiday notebook

Travels in Belgium and Germany, in a party of 4, afterwards increased to 8
August – September 1874

Tuesday August 18
Travelled to London alone; went by express, plucking a feather from the wing of time according to the most modern and luxurious fashion. Left heavy impedimenta at Euston and wrote directly for its delivery in Wiesbaden. Cabbed to Hilldrop and spent night with Frank B and Edwin H.

Wednesday August 19
Frank and I left Charing Cross about 7 am. and soon arrived on Dover pier. Running down to the steamboat we descried Mr and Mrs Briggs already embarked. A wave of the hat soon followed by hearty hand shaking introduced the travelling party to one another.

Bright sun, smooth sea. No striking incident during the voyage to Calais. Aired my French with a Gallic sailor and found it in a decidedly rusty condition.

Calais – Mr B., Frank and I had an enjoyable bathe in the sea. Soft sand and gently sloping shore. Wandered about the quaint old town so long an English possession, but lost by our disreputable Mary. Interesting place. Picturesque old houses and market place. Indulged in an "eclair" first taste of continental luxuries.

Afternoon – took train to Lille . . . Put up at the hotel attached to station. Comfortable. Made our debut in town by gas-light.

Thursday 20
. . . Frank and I bathed in the extensive open-air baths of the town; they are divided out into portions of different depth and are situated in gardens where gymnastic conveniences are also provided for use during nudity . . .

Lille to Tournai

. . . After tea went to the park and had a good specimen of a Belgian's summer evening. A band played very good music in a pavilion, while around in an avenue of trees surrounding a large grass plot, the inhabitants of the town walked and sat and talked, enjoyed the fresh air and the charming music.

Friday 21

Visited the celebrated cathedral of Tournai . . . a building of very large proportions and of imposing aspect . . .

Tournai to Ghent

(Hotel de Vienne, good position, comfortable)

Visited cathedral, St Bavon. Pine interior. Pulpit sculptured partly in wood, partly in marble. Pictures by the Van Eycks . . . etc.

Marche au Vendredi, surrounded by quaint old houses. Here were celebrated with great pomp the entry of the Counts of Flanders, after they had sworn to observe the privilege and liberties of the people. Here the patriotic weavers of Ghent used to meet at the call of Philip of Artevelde and others of their leaders, to maintain their rights and liberties . . . A colossal monument now stands here of Jacques of Artevelde who led the inhabitants when they joined Edward of England against France . . .

Church of St Michel contains paintings by . . . Van der Mander, Van Dyck etc . . . Grand Beguinage, a most interesting and extensive nunnery. Went to Vespers which commence at 7 o'clock. 400-600 nuns with white hoods assembled in church; unique and striking sight. The peculiarity of this institution is that an inmate can leave whenever she likes. It contains about 800, rich and poor, old and young. They say no one ever avails herself of the privilege to leave. They have their private apartments and keep themselves. Some sew, some make lace, some wash[25]. I believe one or two have been there 50-60 years. Some are very rich. The institute is like a small town in itself.

Saturday 22

Ghent to Brussels

Hotel de Hollande. Perambulated the town and went to "la Musique" in the park. Fashionable resort. Good music. Cosmopolitan crowd. Delicious coffee and ices . . .

Monday 24

Frank B and I start early for Antwerp . . . Stayed . . . a few hours, returning to Brussels in the evening . . . Cathedral, Notre Dame. This far famed structure, considered the largest and finest Gothic structure in Belgium, greatly

disappointed me in its exterior appearance. Its single tower looks odd and incomplete without its comrade, and gives to the building a lopsided unsymmetrical appearance which prevents one from admiring many of the artistic beauties which it possesses. The interior however is deserving of the highest praise, the chief attraction being the 7 aisles lined with pillars whose delicate shafts run up into handsome groins in the roof . . .
After taking a tram along the fine new boulevards . . . we took train back to Brussels.

Tuesday 25
. . . Visited the Zoological garden. Good, but not equal to London. Visited the Wiertz gallery[26] of painting, the most interesting I ever saw. Great variety of style. Some very realistic paintings placed so as to take one by surprise at every step. One is kept on the tip-toe of expectation and astonishment at every moment. Rather too much licence of subject matter to gratify an Englishman's idea of chastity . . .

Wednesday August 26
Frank and I went to Louvain and saw its Cathedral . . . perhaps the best type of Gothic architecture in Belgium. It is crowded with pinnacles from top to bottom, and displays an astonishing amount of detail throughout.

Louvain to Namar
. . . Frank availed himself of some excellent baths in the river. Train to Dinant where we met Mr and Mrs B again. Hotel being full (Hotel Tete D'Or. Good.) Frank and I occupied a small room over a grocer's . . .

The next day they all left for Liege and travelled on from there to Bonn

Saturday 29
F. and I left Mr and Mrs B here, and took steamer to Biebrich where we arrived at about 8 pm after 12 hours on the Rhine. (Hotel zurn Baren. Comfortable, very attentive. Mod. charges.) Paid a preliminary visit to Miss Beyerhaus' establishment[27].

Sunday August 30
Went to German church in the morning. Took coffee at Miss B's in the afternoon and then had a walk with Mary and Mima to Sonnenberg. Took them to Eng. church in the evening and then afterwards took tea at Miss B's with the school and family, and sang hymns till about 10.

Monday 31
Drove off from Miss B's in a carriage and pair containing: Flora, Emily, STM, EFAB, Mary and Mima down to Beibrich, took steamer, and after a very fine and most enjoyable 6-7 hours run, amongst the beautiful Rhine scenery, made still more charming by the jovial company, who beguiled the intervals of less interesting localities with jokes and riddles, arrived at Bonn. Here FB, Mary and Emily joined Mr and Mrs B, but Flora, Mima and I went on to Cologne and visited the Cathedral and St Ursula, not omitting to see the relics or to buy some E de C. Returned to Bonn by train and found Mr B etc . . . awaiting us. Defiled in one combination to the Rheineck Hotel.

Tuesday September 1
The now complete and very merry party of 8 took early steamer to Remagen. Here after terrible haggling with incomprehensible drivers we took two carriages and drove up the Ahr valley . . . on to Attenahr the mountains increased in height and presented some very fine points of view. The abrupt hillsides were thickly covered with vineyards or dense woods. The road winding in and out amongst the spars of rocks presented constantly varying landscapes.

Attenahr
Rested our horses 2 hours and dined. Returned to Remagen, our company dividing differently. On the way I was happy to espy some mistletoe in an apple tree. Descended from the carriage like a thunderbolt, clambered up the tree, and returned bearing the valuable trophy.

The steamer to Bonn coming up as soon as we arrived at the landing stage, our coachman succeeded in swingling us out of a Thaler or so.

Returned to Bonn, and after meeting, (a larky rather than solemn conclave) in Mr B's bedroom to arrange for tomorrow's proceedings, retired to bed. (This parliamentary gathering took place regularly every night, our movements being decided frequently by vote.)

Wednesday September 2
Mary, Mima and I visited the Chemical Lab. which is reached by the pretty Popplesdorf Avenue. Frank, Flora and Emily visited a museum meanwhile . . . About midday the six repaired to a photographer's and had their six noble countenances and their half-dozen elegant figures combinely represented on paper.

Holiday photograph taken on September 2nd. 1874 in Bonn.
Left to right – standing . . . Theodore, Flora.
Seated . . . Emily Lloyd, Mary (in hat), Arthur Briggs and Mima.

Returned to hotel. Dined. Embarked on steamer and shortly after landed at Konigswinter. Ascended in the company of two donkeys to the elevated summit of the Drachenfelz. Were duly crowned en route by a fair maiden with wreathes of oak leaves.

On the summit, our desire for adventure began to be indulged. Mima, Flora, Frank and I stood on the ever memorable ledge of a rock projecting over a perpendicular precipice. Our foolhardy temerity led us to within a very hair's breadth of the edge. On descending we each (the 4) purchased an exceedingly bad photo of the "Memorable ledge." Took tea on the top, and astonished other visitors by our extremely mercurial and boisterous behaviour.

Descended to Konigswinter. Had to wait in the dusk on the river-side some half hour before the steamer arrived. Enlivened the time and no doubt bewildered the numerous bystanders by loud solo and choral singing, "Rule Britannia" may be mentioned. At the conclusion Frank's courage failed him and he wouldn't take the hat round.

Returned by steamer to Bonn, singing and being sung to by some Germans, all the way. Anniversary of Sedan, much cannon firing. After tea armed the ladies into the market place to see the fireworks etc.

The solemnity of the bedroom Parliament was somewhat disturbed by an unexpected occurrence.

The ladies on leaving the room were discovered beneath a bough of mistletoe mischievously hung in their way by some sly individual. The result was that sundry of them received sweet impressions on their soft cheeks, which we hope left sweet impressions on their gentle minds.

Thursday September 3

The immortal party of 8 now embarked early on board a large steamer . . . Wended our merry way down the German Rhine . . . passing Drachenfelz . . . Remagen . . . through the bridge of boats under the frowning fortress of Ehrenbrechstein at Coblentz . . . to St Goar . . . Poured like a tidal wave into the Rheinfelz Hotel. By the way, Mary and I were very nearly carried on by the steamer beyond our goal, for searching after an unlucky umbrella belonging, be it noticed, to Mima, we found the landing board removed when we arrived on deck. It was no doubt the aristocratic appearance of our party that induced the angry captain to put us on shore.

Umbrella casualties:-

Flora ingeniously left hers at Attenahr and so unburdened herself for the whole outing. Mima now slyly contrived to follow her example; I was so foolish as to keep mine all the time and wear it out completely without using it.

Having deposited our baggage in the hotel we took the delightful little steam ferry across to St Goarhausen . . . Mima, Flora and I wandered on a long way before the others. Deep in conversation we noticed neither time nor space and at length found ourselves in the remote village of Bornich. After a quarter of an hours rest we returned to find our comrades, who likewise sent out a party to seek us. Once more together we descended by a wild and perilous path of our own formation to the Rhine . . . Walked back round the Lorelei corner, proved the perfection of the celebrated echo, and finally reached the ferry some time after dark.

After tea we made the hotel resound with merry English songs . . .

Friday September 4

Paid a visit to the extensive ruin of Reinfelz. Found a most entertaining cicerone over it. He took us by means of a ladder to the highest pinnacle, and there we stayed to Mr and Mrs B's horror, and the amazement of individuals some hundreds of perpendicular feet below, and sang "Heil, Kaiser, Dir!" . . . Dined. Took ferry again to St Goarhausen. Entered the Patersberg valley. (Mrs B being unwell remained behind.)

In perhaps 2 hours we reached a village on the table-land above the Rhine. Here our folly culminated. The 7 of us arm in arm in one long row marched twice through the village shouting our wild native songs. With regard to the effect on the inhabitants, cannot say more than that they were utterly stupefied.

Returning, Mima, Flora and I again managed to elude our comrades and presently found ourselves at the top of a steep precipitous descent, in a most desolate region, and night fast closing in. While I reconnoitred the girls sat down and rested. Then by slow stages, I leading them each alone, we gradually descended into the gloomy valley below us. Here we heard our comrades' voices singing "See our oars" in the far distance; we therefore dived into some brushwood on the edge of a forest, and remained concealed till all danger of a rencontre had disappeared. Then arm in arm we descended the dark valley, and after an hour's walk reached the Rhine. Here our adventure was nearly spoiled, for on descending to the ferry we heard our comrades already on board. Under cover of the night we retreated however and took a short parade on the bank. Looking over the river to the ferry boat that landed our party on the other side, we were horrified to see the lights thrown overboard, and the boat left motionless at the further bank. Descending at once to the water side we tolled a solemn bell, and soon to our relief a man appeared, and rowed us across.

Arrived at the hotel we found further excitement awaiting us. I went up into the ladies bedroom to ask my two companions their orders for tea. Now these two had rather exasperated Mary by a determined silence and mysteriousness with regard to our evening's experience. Mary therefore took the opportunity of shutting me in, locking the door and leaving. Finding myself in this awkward predicament I hauled at the bell-rope perhaps too vigorously. Presently the door opened and I beheld the hotel keeper, the head-waiter and the boots standing aghast. The loud ringing had terrified them, and the sudden collapse of excitement now rather awoke their wrath, the waiter crossly remarking that I evidently wanted a whole house for myself.

However I made it up with him after, and when we had finished tea, we again woke the echoes through-out the remotest and most spider afflicted corners of the hotel. "Auld Lang Syne" having been given in one form, and then the solemn setting of the nocturnal Parliament being accomplished, we retired to dream how the lines had fallen to us in very pleasant places.

Saturday 5

Directly after breakfast scaled the heights behind the town and attained the lofty table-land through which the Rhine has worn so deep a hollow.

Descending took the steamer . . . reached Biebrich as the mountain shadows were fast lengthening into general gloom on the Rhine.

Two carriages to No. 3 Hainer Weg, where Fraulein Maria greedily welcomed back the charming quarternion. Fraulein Maria, I must confess, behaved very well during all my experience of her, nearly always yielding to our wishes and ever shewing an eager interest in our enjoyment. Of course the girls liked to speak of her as possessing qualities which usually pertain to a vulture, eagle or other ravenous bird of prey; but happily I only felt the soft plumage and not the sharp talons.

Sunday 6
German church, morning. The 8 walked to Sonnenburg in the afternoon. The 8 took tea in the Bear Hotel after having attended service in the English church. The 4 escorted the 4 back to their nest. Extracted (the method of attack was planned beforehand) and without difficulty, a promise that we might enjoy the company of the 4 downy and charming eaglets all the next day, providing Mr and Mrs B were of the party.

Monday 7
Two carriages to the Platte . . . Look over the Platte house, dined, wandered away in the woods, returned singing by the Neroberg through the woods to Wiesbaden on foot.

Tuesday
Mr and Mrs Briggs and F. Briggs depart for England, I go with them a day's journey. Touching farewell scene at Miss B's.

Melancholy drive to Biebrich. Vainly strive to be merry by singing on the boat. Stay at the Victoria Hotel, Bingen. Hypochondria is chronic and reaches its climax. Take an evening walk, Mr B, Frank and I, but find it a failure; decidedly in the dumps.

Wednesday 9
Train early on to Treves, I accompany them as far as Kreuznach. A grasp of the hand, a word, a hat waved, and they are gone . . . Train to Bingen.

I ascend to the Rochuscapelle . . . Dine at the Victoria. Take a boat to Assmanshausen. Walk over the lovely Niederwald . . . down the other side to Rudesheim . . . Arrived in Wiesbaden, pay a nocturnal visit to Miss B's to see for letters. Hear Flora's merry voice echoing beyond the panes of her bedroom window; hold surreptitious converse with M and M through their bedroom window, they being I believe in the last stages of evening toilette.

Repair to the Bear.

Hotel zum Baren, Wiesbaden. September 10 1874
My dear Father,

. . . Mr and Mrs Briggs have gone . . . I returned here last night and expecting a communication from you went straight away to Hainer Weg and had a nocturnal communication with Mary and Mima through their bedroom window.

I've been settling up cash this morning and overhauling my luggage. I find I've spent $32, leaving $18 to go on with. All things included, the average has been about $1 a day for myself for 22 days = $22, and 17s per day for each of the two girls for 6 days = $10 and we've had our money's worth I assure you. A jollier, merrier, more enjoyable week of its kind we never spent.

I'm going to settle with Flora and Emily today I hope. It has cost them about $5 a piece, Emily rather under . . .

I hear that M and M have given you a detailed account of our proceedings, so I will forbear to recall memories past, alas for ever. The reaction setting in naturally makes one rather mopish but I'll try to enjoy the merry retrospect and look to its repetition some day . . .

Just received your letter from Morecombe. It makes me more undecided than before. At Zurich they speak abominable German, in fact Miss Maria Beyerhaus says she can't understand them.

I enclose Dr. Hofmann's last letter. He suggests Hanover but says that any good lab. would do. So I think that it would be best to go as first proposed to Berlin. The German spoken there is moderately good though not up to Hanover German . . .

Mary received letters from Mama and Nellie this morning.

Many thanks and much love from all to all. In haste,

Your very affectionate son, Theo Mander.

Hotel zum Baren, Wiesbaden September 11 1874[28]

My dear Father,

This morning I called on Dr. Remigius Fresnius, Professor of Chemistry in Wiesbaden. He is a jolly old fellow and moreover, a man of wide renown for his chemical learning. I asked his advice with regard to myself, after having laid my position before him. It is to go to any good organic chemist and he mentioned as the two most eligible Dr. Hofmann of Berlin and Prof. Kekule of Bonn. He advises more especially the latter because he is a first rate organic chemist and would be more likely to give me special attention than Dr. Hofmann, since the latter being a large city, probably has his mind filled with a variety of subjects and his time occupied with many different persons. Two of Dr. Fresnius' pupils who have gone to Bonn tell him that Prof. Kekule is constantly in the laboratory . . . Kolbe at Leipsig is a good organic chemist. Prof. Krau of Hanover is a good man but too far away. Prof. Bunsen at Heidelburg is a good chemist but very old and devoted to inorganic studies. Prof. Kopp of Zurich is a good practical chemist but chiefly skilled in aniline colours . . . Dr. Fresnius says that he knows of no chemist who has specially studied in my line and that a good organic chemist like Hofmann or Kekule would be the man for me. I spoke about the skill of Hofmann's assistant who has lately discovered the method for making vanilla from gum. The Dr. said he is probably a private assistant of the Professor's . . . Professor Fresnius himself has 5 or 6 private assistants and only 3 to teach his students. It seems now to be a question of the balance of advantages between Berlin and Bonn. . . Berlin . . . possesses the usual advantages of a metropolis and our agents are there. Again Bonn is prettily situated and Berlin has most uninteresting suburban country. I believe the German at Bonn is moderately good.

I propose remaining here in Wiesbaden till the middle of next week, that I may hear from you. I can see Robert Felkin conveniently to him any time during the next 3 weeks and can also occupy my time here . . . though it's very uninteresting sightseeing alone. The girls will probably not begin work for another week so I can see them occasionally. They will probably have tea with me this evening at the hotel (ie Mary and Mima) Unfortunately proprieties prevent me from having the other two. Perhaps we shall go to a concert too this afternoon. I took my photograph and scrap albums in to Miss Beyerhaus' last night and had a jolly evening with all the girls that are left there.

I hope you are all of you much the better for the seaside visit.

Very much love to all, ever your affectionate son, Theo Mander.

PS What do you think about my absence from home? Wouldn't it be a pity to run too great risks with regard to the knowledge of manufacture being in so few hands?

Hotel zum Baren, Wiesbaden September 16 1874
My dear Father,

Received yours this morning. Thank you very much especially for advice and prayers. I intend leaving here tomorrow on the way to Chemnitz. I shall stop the night at Eisenach and see the Wartburg where Luther was confirmed and translated so much of the Bible. I expect to stay a few days in Chemnitz with Robert and then go to Berlin. There I hope to see Dr. Hofmann. I shall then be better able to decide on any further movements . . .

I shall reduce expenses by travelling 3rd class. Distances are tremendous.

I think I shall forward herewith a statement of my finances and expenses. I fear it will show a necessity for reinforcement though I don't think I have been extravagant:-

	£	s	d
August 18 to September 16 – travelling and hotel expenses ...	23	4	0
Luggage – London to Wiesbaden		17	0
Mary and Mima – 6 days travelling and one or two other excursions	9	13	5
Spent myself on private a/c, eg photos, presents, including £2 spent towards clothes before starting	5	10	7

In hand 10 15 0

50 0 0

You will see that the first two items together on 29 days only averages 16/6 per day.

Could I have some more money please at Chemnitz? for though the amount in hand may last from 10 days to a fortnight, it is very uncomfortable and sometimes awkward to run low.

Would you send it me (by return) to Poste Restante or:-

R.W. Felkin, Nicolai Graben 81, Chemnitz. Saxony.

With very much love to yourself, dear Mama and all, ever your affectionate son, Theo Mander.

Diary

Thursday September 17
Last evening bid adieu to No 3 Hainer Weg. Leave luggage at Bear Hotel. Train to Eisennach.

Stayed at a very German Inn where no English was known. Perambulated the streets of this quiet old town by gas-light. Had nothing but a heavy duvet for bedcover for first time. No sheet on top.

Friday September 18
Rose early and ascended the Wartburg. The exquisite scenery was rendered still more enjoyable by the variegated autumn foliage of the trees, and the delicious odours with which decaying vegetation pervaded the atmosphere . . .

Train to Erfurt . . .

Visited Cathedral with very unusual double portal. Interesting interior . . .

Train to Leipzig

Saturday 19 Hotel de Prusse
. . . Interesting but very shabby town. Not one fine looking building. Some large ones but of poor architecture and all plastered. Focus of German book trade. Saw – Theatre, Museum of Pictures, Chemical Lab., (largest in Germany) Booksellers' Bourse . . . Promenade on old ramparts round the town . . .

September 19-24
With Robert Felkin in Chemnitz, a very pleasant enjoyable visit . . . Visited Sachsische Maschinen-Fabrik, one of the largest works of the sort on the Continent. Order and economy of space very noticeable . . .

Spent Tuesday together in Leipzig. One of the 3 great annual Leipzig fairs. Didn't go to bed all night. Prowled about the town and sat in cafés, till 4 am when the last we could find was closed. Returned to Chemnitz about 6 am.

Thursday September 24
Train to Dresden . . .

Saturday 26
Dresden to Berlin travelling the waste-howling wilderness which for 40 – 50 miles or more surrounds the capital . . .

Sunday September 27
. . . Called on Mr Davies[29] pm; took tea with him and accompanied him in evening to most interesting free-discussion Bible-class at American chapel.

Hotel de Baviere, Hamburg Sunday October 4 1874
My very dear Father,

You will probably be rather surprised to see my heading and perhaps more surprised to hear what follows. Since I wrote you last from Berlin I have visited Mr Davies and Messrs Meissner and Schuster. They have all been very kind to me. The first named gentleman invited me to tea with him and his wife (German) on Sunday evening and I went with him to a Bible-class of Eng. and Americans afterwards. There I met Mr Root, an American who has much assisted me . . . I have seen Berlin pretty well, for I was persuaded to remain there till Friday . . . Before I left Berlin, I spent an hour with a friend of Mr Roots', an American also, who has studied (chemistry) a considerable time with Prof. Hofmann and before that in several Labs in America. He also knows fellows who have studied in Bonn and elsewhere. The result of my interview with him has been to decide me finally to remain under Dr. Hofmann in Berlin . . .

According to my lights before, Bonn seemed most eligible. But I felt a Divine guidance that night, taking me to Mr Roots' where I met his friend. This gentleman's testimony I have no reason to doubt.

Dr. Hofmann he says, is altogether a first class man, the best man undoubtedly for research in Germany (and my work must be research) A good theoretical man, more practical than either Kekule or Kraut. He is twice every day in the Lab going round to the fellows. He questions tremendously and makes his pupils thoroughly understand what they are about. He is well up in every branch of chemistry, and in chemical debates with other professors is ready to answer any one of them on any subject. He has probably done as much or more in any way than any one else.

Prof. Kraut is a great theorist and is now very much taken up with editing books etc.

Prof. Kekule is a fearful theorist and has gone now very much into physics. Also this American hears that he comes often into the Lab at the commencement of the term, but afterwards is very lax in his attendance . . .

On the whole I think Dr. Hofmann who is a very sensible, learned, thorough man, will possess for me the best combination of theoretical and practical knowledge . . . They say any work requires 3 or 4 years at least. However more than one is impossible. I should be very glad to come home and help you any day; though I do appreciate my advantages. I feel considerably homesick sometimes.

I stayed a day in Hanover and saw it pretty well. Liked it much. Came on here last night . . . Like this place immensely. Its a sort of mixture of Liverpool and Amsterdam. I feel at home where there is plenty of smoke and activity.

. . . Perhaps tomorrow I shall take a steamer to Heligoland, returning next day and then straight back to Berlin. Am reading as much German as I can. Find it becoming much easier. Am quite ready to get to work hard.

Very much love to all . . . Ever your loving son Theodore.

Have travelled third class several times but in journeys of 5 or 6 hours it makes one's spine ache uncommonly.

Diary

Tuesday 6
Started early by steamer for Heligoland . . .

Had a very fine view of the animated docks and harbour of Hamburg, the charm of the scene being increased by the bright morning sun. The right bank of the Elbe is at first lined with woods, but the land gradually retreats and the trees disappear, till . . . we touch at Cuxhaven, and then enter the open sea. The motion of our small vessel now became strong enough to cause me to remain immovable on a sofa in the cabin with a book. This was entirely a measure of self defence. Passed the low flat island of Neuwerk with lighthouse. The sea now became so rough that our captain would not trust our frail bark to its mercy, and so we turned back to Cuxhaven. In this small, bleak, uninteresting spot I and two Austrians passed the night. Discovered a Scotch captain and crew in the little port who had put in to repair a leakage after a heavy storm. I believe there were several English vessels there . . .

Wednesday 7
Wind much stronger. Returned by another boat to Hamburg . . . Dined at Hotel de Baviere and returned by express in 6-7 hours to Berlin . . .

By Mr Meissner's kind assistance, soon found comfortable lodgings in a first-class pension, Zelten 18, with fine look-out over the Thiergarten.

Huddersfield October 13th 1874
My dear Theodore,

You see we are at the Congregational Union meetings, we – for I have brought your Mama with me – came in at 10.30 last night. After the morning conference we go to Manchester to attend another meeting of the United Alliance (Permissive Bill) in the Free Trade Hall. Back tomorrow morning and home in the evening . . . Your various letters have much interested and quite satisfied me. All you have done I quite approve though I confess I regret I suggested third class travelling. How is the spine? If it hurts you, if there is an aching and fatigue at the base of the column, consult a skilled medical man at once. It may need rest or . . . bathing or something else; but give it immediate attention . . .

I do not think the amount you are going to pay . . . at all excessive. Should think the Thiergarten a very desirable neighbourhood from my recollections. The best indeed. Am much obliged to Messrs. M. and S. and will write them my thanks. Must close immediately – after breakfast to go to meeting. Will write again. Money a/c quite satisfactory. Love, affectionately yours S.S. Mander.

Frau Vorwerk, Zelten 18. Berlin. October 18 1874 Sunday afternoon
My dear Father,

I must just write a weekly letter before I finish preparing for our Bible discussion class. It is my turn to conduct it tonight . . .

Last Friday evening I went to an American's, a Dr. Eastlake. There were about 15 Americans and English there, mostly American. This meeting occurs weekly for practising psalmody in order that the singing may go better and more heartily in the Church. Mrs Eastlake is . . . very talkative and lively and merry and happy; determined to make everyone else so too. She makes one at home at once.

I am taking German lessons now from an English man who speaks German nearly as well as English, having had all his education in Bonn. I think this is the best plan at first. When I understand German better I intend to get a German to teach me, one who knows no English would be best. I'm getting on pretty well I think and am very happy. . . I have not got my luggage yet but expect it every day from Wiesbaden. Thank you very much for your last letter, Mama and Lottie also. I'm so glad you enjoyed the Oxford meetings so much . . . (they) seem to have been the means of much blessing. I wish there was some such spirit here amongst the Germans . . .

I had a ride the other day with a fellow in this pension. They can be had for 3/- each . . .

I had to get 150 Thalers from M. and S. the other day for board and lodging, college fees, lectures and laboratory. Of course it won't cost all that . . .

Ever affectionate son, Theo Mander

P.S. Sunday evening 10 o'clock

Just returned from the Bible class which has been most interesting. Met a gentleman about 55 apparently, from Birmingham, who knew the name of Mander, Japan manufacturer. He made some very nice remarks . . .

Zelten 18, Berlin October 26 1874

My very dear Father,

Many thanks for your last and for Mama's . . .

I went to the Laboratory this morning, the opening day. Lectures commence tomorrow. Saw Dr. Hofmann who was very pleasant, seems quite to approve of my coming and found me a place at once in the Inorganic Lab. The Organic Lab is full so I shall have rather farther to walk to do my combustions. Otherwise this circumstance is, I believe, an advantage for in the Organic Lab there are several English and Americans, whereas in the Inorganic Lab I hear there are not any[30]. The two rooms are connected with a passage in which a good deal of our work will be done.

If you have not sent the gums, will you please send them at once . . . I had better have some of each sort of gum also some oil, a little litharge may as well be put in too. Would you also have put in a platinum dish and a box of weights which will be found in the small locked drawer in the Laboratory at the Works. Unfortunately I have the key and the lock is patent but if it cannot be opened otherwise, it would be worthwhile breaking the lock, for the plat. dish is worth at least £2 and the box of weights £1.10s. I don't want to have to buy more here . . .

Please enclose a "Euclid" from my bedroom and Valentine's "Qualitative Analysis" perhaps in my bedroom, but more probably in the Works in one of the drawers . . .

The most earnest religious fellow I know is a Scotsman, son of the Rev. Alexander Mackay, of the Free Church of Scotland. Do you know the name?

. . . You ask what the course of study is. I simply attend lectures by Dr. Hofmann three days a week and work in the Lab the rest of the time, viz 3-5 daily. Saturday 9-2. Lectures 9-11. I commence by learning to make a combustion, ie – to estimate amounts of oxygen, hydrogen and carbon in a substance, those being probably the only constituents of the substances I have to do with. This being learnt, I pass the substance experiment on, through various processes and make complete analyses very frequently to ascertain the change it has undergone.

. . . I must really close now. Letter writing employs too much of my time.

. . . Much love to everyone at home. Believe me, your ever loving son,

Theo Mander.

Extract from accounts for October

	Th.	Gr.
Board and lodging. October 12 – November 9	50	0
13th. Washing	1	24
14th. Matriculation at University..	6	0

15th. Copy books	0	22 ½
17th. Reading room (6 months)	2	0
Part of ride (extra)	0	15
21st. Laboratory Practice and Hofmann's lectures	39	20
Luggage from Wiesbaden	2	7
Station to house	0	25
24th. 8 German lessons	5	10
German Grammar	1	20
Fee at Laboratory	1	0½
	124	23 ½

Diary

November 21st
Mary and Mima are now in Wiesbaden, Nellie in London, Howard in Manchester, I in Berlin. Dear parents, Lottie and Martin in Wolverhampton.

Berlin November 22nd 1874
My very dear Father,

Much obliged for bill of Lading. Will look after the case. Very much interested in Gladstone's pamphlet and the letters it has called forth . . .

I will ride out as often as I can but three times a week is scarcely possible as it is dark long before I leave the Laboratory. My eyes have been rather painful lately. Hurt me to read long also other times so I thought it advisable to visit a good oculist. My eyes have been more or less troublesome for two years. The oculist gave me prescriptions for eye water, to wash my face with also and for eye salve. He says it is nothing serious but a scrofulous affection of the eyes (and) of the eyelids.

. . . What are Moody and Sankey doing now? How goes the revival in England and Scotland? How are Uncle Charles and Uncle Harper? In haste and with very much love to you and Mama. Ever your affectionate son,
Theo Mander.

Diary

December 3
Went to see a German boar hunt in the Grunewald. Was introduced there with companions, to Prince Carl.

Berlin December 7 1874
My dear Father,

. . . I went down to the station this morning and ascertained details regarding time, tickets, sleeping cars etc. I calculate by the daily through Europe Express, with sleeping car to the Russian frontier (it is not admitted further at present) we could spend a good time in St Petersburg being back in Berlin in 14 days, for £20 a piece. I am aware of the character of a Russian winter and am sure shall be able to make suitable provision against it. St Petersburg ought to be seen in winter much rather than summer for the sake of its world renown skating, sleighing etc. With good introductions that I can get, I think we should spend the time well and I should benefit in many ways by the excursion. I know its a great deal I'm asking but its on the plea of this being a special year . . .

Our holidays are from December 20 to January 4th, or some say January 7th. Would you please answer soon that I may have thick top coat made and get a fur for the neck if I may go.

Believe me ever your affectionate son, Theo Mander.

Zelten 18, Berlin December 1874
My very dear Father,

Thank you very much for the permission to go to St Petersburg. Do you know I now fear the journey will not come off. For such a long journey we should be at least four to enjoy it thoroughly. My American friend Simpson on second thoughts, and on reckoning his past expenses, finds he cannot go. Mrs Fox has been very ill and is recovering slowly so that Mr Fox cannot go. Myers would still go but we can find no one else, also we read in the papers that it is quite mild in St Petersburg. Under these circumstances we should not derive half the possible enjoyment or benefit from the tour and therefore it would be both a waste of time and money to undertake it. It's a great disappointment. However I shall feel freer to travel a bit when I go down, D.V. to Vienna. Thank you very much all the same for the permission and Mama for her good motherly letter. I must write to thank Mr Pozanaski for his invitation . . .

Last Thursday I went to a genuine German party at Herr Loesche's. There were about twenty there, all Germans but myself, an American and two Japanese. I did a wonderful amount of German conversation. Herr L. seems to move in good circles, his house also is very well furnished. He and his son occupy the whole which is rare here. The German customs are very different from the English. There is an immense amount of formality with them. The chief peculiarity of this evening was that we did nothing the whole time. Herr Loesche does not allow dancing in his house I was glad to hear . . . This evening . . . It snows a la Russe . . .

Chemistry I get very tired of sometimes, it's such dirty work and gums are such a tedious thankless subject. I don't know whether this Chemistry exam of them will be much use. I think the practical experience of a workshop . . . far more likely to be useful . . .

I don't wish to imply that Berlin is not the best place for me of any continental lab. I think most probably it is . . .

Now with much love . . . I am your affectionate son, Theo Mander.

December 8 Tuesday
. . . Take more constant care to be ever near God . . . Let mind be ever under Divine influence. Let heart be ever in Heaven. Let amusement be a rational exercise for mind or body. Be in the world not of the world . . .

Berlin December 1874
My dear Father,

. . . This semester ends in the middle of March . . . and the next term commences at the end of April . . . I think this semester will be enough for me here don't you? Then, don't you think to carry out your idea, I might do a month's varnishing here till middle of April, then go to Vienna and do practical work there again, till about the end of May; then, perhaps do a little travelling and finally reach Paris in time to do a month or six weeks practical varnishing and return home in beginning of August. This would just complete the year.

Xmas is now almost here and the earth has already donned her white robe . . .

The streets now swarm with buyers, public places are all choked with a plethora of Xmas trees, the shop windows exhibit vast arrays of turkeys, geese, attractive pastry inventions etc. and the centre of the town is occupied by a vast Xmas fair. One thing is lacking. Mistletoe is unknown here.

Now wishing you all a very happy, merry Christmas, I remain ever your very affectionate son, Theo Mander.

Zelten 18, Berlin December 27 1874
My very dear Father,

Sunday afternoon.

Robert and I sitting in my room both writing home. He came yesterday after being delayed seven hours over the usual time on the road, by the heavy snows. Passengers had to get out and help clear snow from before the engine and in one place were conveyed on in sledges . . .

On Xmas Eve, 8 of us from the pension made a sledge expedition with two sledges and four horses. We went to Spandow and back, about 16 miles.

The snow lies here about four inches thick and it has frozen more or less for a week. There are many sledges about now. Some private ones are very neat turnouts.

On returning on Wednesday we had a grand Xmas tree in the pension, all lodgers bringing their gifts with them. After that ceremony (a very important and imposing one in every house here) they danced a great part of the evening. I, however, went to see another Xmas tree in the heart of a genuine German family, viz Herr Loesche's. Here the exhibition of presents was preceded by a hymn and chapter of the Bible.

On Xmas day I went to dinner at a Miss Harper's at three. We were ten English ladies and gentlemen, one American and one Dutchman. Here we had a good English carouse, so to speak. Turkey and fiery plum pudding around the table . . . warmed the cockles of our hearts with physical heat and remembrance of home.

After dinner some Germans came in and we had a jolly afternoon together.

At about six o'clock Mackay, Root and I went down to Mr Davies' who had just had a Xmas tree for cabmen's wives and children. We came in for the end and then spent a very pleasant evening there with five English ladies. We had some Scotch songs and closed with singing, reading and prayer. Mr D. had some mistletoe and holly over from England . . .

You asked me what I have done in linseed oil and turpentine. Nothing at all . . . The experiments which I should like to perform as bearing on your difficulties, and likely directly or indirectly to give some solution of the problem, I cannot perform here because I should at once make dangerous revelations and suggestions to my professors and fellow students. For instance, I should like to study the changes that the gums may undergo, varying conditions of temperature, exposure and surrounding air, but this I don't like to do because, as you say, it would all remain in the professor's mind . . .

As to bloom and cracking, I think one could better experiment on them in John Street[31] than here. Not only would there be more privacy but also more suitable facilities . . .

Please thank Howard very much for his letter. Nellie also. Lottie likewise. Very much love to all and wishes for a very happy new year, also from Robert. Your very loving son, Theodore Mander.

Extract from accounts for December[32]

	Th	Gr
December 1 – January 1 Board and Lodging	50	0
Breakages, Heating etc	7	19
Apparatus and chemicals at Laboratory	20	9½
Blue spectacles for Lab	0	20
December 3 – My portion of carriage for the hunt	1	11
15 100 visiting cards	1	15
Writing paper	1	8
Supper at hotel with Meissner and Co	0	20
21 – Xmas box to sick porter of our house	2	0
22 – Xmas boxes to our 3 servants	4	0
Pair of kid fur-lined gloves	2	20
Longfellow	0	12

24 – Smiles' "Character" in German (present)	2	10
Xmas bouquet for Frau Loesche	3	0
December 28 – Portion of sledge drive (3 of us treated the Vorwerks)	4	7
Third of Xmas present given by English lodgers to Frau Vorwerk	8	20
	131	3

Diary

December 31st Thursday
Last day of an eventful year . . . As I sit in my room tonight I hear the dancing and excitement of my fellow lodgers underneath . . .

Berlin tonight is full of balls; public and private dancing celebrates the changing year. At Krolls there is a masked ball. I thank God for the dancing within that I experience.

Diary

January 1st Friday 1875
Year opened with propitious feelings in my heart, faith, love, confidence give me new happiness.

Had two to three hours skating this morning amongst the hundreds at the Russel Insel.

Good letter from Mary and pleasant visit from Mackay . . .

January 10th Sunday
Gave away about 30 Gospels with tracts in each. Mackay and I have commenced this distribution every Sunday to cabmen . . .

Zelten 18, Berlin. January 10th 1875
My very dear Father,

Your welcome letter received last Wednesday and Mama's . . .

I should think your plan for Nellie and Lottie is likely to be very satisfactory, especially for the latter. Nellie has had a good spell at Mrs Gill's and I daresay the change will be good for her. The society and the distance and the novelty will, I've no doubt, greatly benefit Lottie. It will be difficult to find a more beautiful spot than Miss Hooper's school on the continent. The lovely blue lake stretching right and left from the front of the house, its edge only separated from the building by a narrow garden. The gigantic snow covered Dent-on-Mur and its neighbours forming the eastern landscape . . . To the west, in the far distance lies Geneva, but I think it's never visible from Vevey. Behind are mountains too

. . . There is a bathing place within a few yards of the school and boats are plentiful.

I enclose my money account from the time I settled in Berlin (October 9th) til December 31st. I find I have spent a tremendous amount, the average being just the same as when I was travelling. Items add up in a wonderful manner.

The fees I have paid at the Laboratory extend, I believe, til the end of the winter semester, March 9th.

I find it more profitable to read at my lodgings now than go to the Laboratory. I am reading a book by Mulder, a Dutchman (German translation.) It is called "The Chemistry of Drying Oils" and contains an elaborate chemical investigation of the exact nature of linseed oil, its behaviour under various circumstances, and its technical application . . . I . . . intend reading up all I can find on oils (and) gums in the Laboratory library . . .

It seems to me that the best thing I can do would be to study all that has already been discovered and done on the subject and then soon to get into a coach builders yard and master as far as possible, in the time, the practical application of the varnishes. . . This week we've had a most interesting series of special prayer meetings. Every evening they were held. We also had three evenings at the American chapel. I went to five . . . Pastor Baur, cathedral preacher, on Saturday delivered a very earnest address . . . Before Pastor Baur, Pastor Pank gave a telling account of his visit to the Oxford Meeting and his general impression of religion in England, especially our strict observance of the Sabbath. He saw that on one occasion, in an English town, the only persons he met with who were openly disregarding the sanctity of the day were a party of his own countrymen . . .

We are having bright, frosty weather, skating but no sledging. Snow has mostly gone.

Now much love to all, from your ever loving son, Theo Mander.

Diary

January 17th Sunday

. . . Some days ago conversed with Herman Vorwerk on religion. He does not believe anything is to be gained by prayers, churchgoing etc. Says he believes he will gain a happy future by steadiness and honesty in business. Has not read the Bible since he was a boy of 12 or 14 when he was forced to use it at school. Never prays I fancy and never attends divine worship. Believes in God and scarcely knows whether he believes in Christ. This sad case is a single example of thousands of such heathens here. I should think there are far more heathens in Berlin than in Antananarivo.

Some weeks ago I had a religious conversation with Emmerling, a student at the Lab. He disclosed after some time the wildness of his professed views on

Man and Time. He said he believed we are all developed from an original germ etc. etc. Darwinism. All the wonders and mysteries of our being to be explained by natural laws. Believed soul to be a movement of matter; natural death spiritual death, therefore no immortality for us; nature to be God; the Bible a mere history of the Jews! This is but one of a large class of student infidels I believe.

Theodore in Berlin

Zelten 18 Berlin January 24th 1875
My dear Father,

It is nearly six o'clock on Sunday afternoon . . . Darkness covers the earth and conceals a wet and muddy scene of melting snow . . . My silent room is illuminated by the soft rays of a solitary petroleum lamp that stands alone in the dusky shades on its one leg . . . In the far corner the red cinders in a stove penetrate the mystic gloom with their genial rays and give the room an air of English comfort . . . A lady below beguiles the hours of deepening twilight with sweet strains of music that ascend on the ethereal wave like angelic messengers . . .

I have a special mention to make of . . . Mackay[33] to you, by his request, as I told him you were a country director of the London Missionary Society.

Mackay is a little fellow, in age 25 . . . He loses no opportunity of doing good here in Berlin. He is at present working in a machine manufactory as designer. He has for some time desired to give himself up to missionary work and that in Madagascar. His particular desire is to go there somewhat as medical missionaries work, only not with a knowledge of medicine but of science generally, either to teach it or to practice it in irrigation, sanitation or carrying out of any engineering works which might become feasible. He would preach as often as possible and make everything subservient to the Gospel work. The people now are open to civilization, increased knowledge of science, and learning generally is sure to come and how important it is that it should be introduced with a good bias and under Christian auspices . . .

Mackay wants to go out under the auspices of the Society and yet to be free to use his judgement and not to be hampered by strict directions as to the exact course he is to pursue. If you approve of the idea, and can give it any support by your influence . . . as a director, Mackay would be thankful.

Monday morning. I have just received the sad and sudden news of Mr Briggs' death . . . I never less expected a death before. The burden falls early on Frank but he seems (to) have firm confidence in unseen powers to uphold him. I hear Mr B. died happily and peacefully though neither Mrs B or Frank were present . . . This event is so sudden and unexpected that I cannot at all realise it yet. I had naturally expected him to live many years more. Well, it does but add another friend to those awaiting on the further shore . . . Mr Meissner has spoken to one of his customers, a first class coach builder here and the latter will be very willing for me to work at his place. I hope to begin next Monday.

We have had a little more snow and frost but now it is mild again . . .

With very much love to Mama, Nellie, Lottie, How and Martin. I am ever your affectionate son, Theo Mander.

Berlin February 6 1875

My dear Father,

I write again to mention an invitation I received from Mr Schuster this morning.

He wants me to join a party of 20 with whom he is going on the 25th of this month down the Danube to Constantinople, Black Sea, Greece, Baalbeck, Jerusalem, all Palestine in fact, Suez Canal, Cairo and the Pyramids. To be back in 3 months at Vienna. Cost £150. At first it seemed good and feasible and I said I would write to you on the subject.

But now I don't think it would be wise to go, even if you were willing to find the money. There will be 2 Russians in the party, the rest Germans from various parts, one a countess and 6 officers.

To spend such a sum and so long a time, one should know one's party well. I don't know any of these except Mr Schuster. The probability is their mode of enjoying travel would be quite different from mine. Sunday would be to them as other days, and the sacred towns of Palestine mere antique curiosities. Such a journey should be with a select party of friends I think, and they of your own nationality. Moreover, this journey would rather interfere with the programme you have given me for the next 5 months. The journey no doubt is a delightful one; Oswald Jackson was describing it to me the other day. He undertook it in a still more extensive form a year or two ago.

I think under the circumstances you will agree with me, and probably will also say, and I agree with you by anticipation, that I had better come home and earn the £150 before I spend it.

If you agree with me will you please give me some proper excuse for Mr Schuster from yourself, as I have already declined an invitation of his to a ball and I fear he will think me unsociable.

Much love to all, from your affectionate son, Theo Mander.

Letter dictated by Samuel Mander[34]

Charing Cross Hotel, London February 22nd 1875
My dear Theodore,

Scarcely had we turned our faces towards London, Wiesbaden and Vevey, when I was reminded of your birthday anniversary, so in hope that this will reach you on the day, Nellie sits down to convey the good wishes which we all cherish and which are prompted by the love we all bear . . . That you should be two and twenty when this letter reaches you is strange to your Mama and me, who remember so well your cradle life. We're thankful whenever we think of you for God's goodness to you and anticipate for you a happy future. But do not for a moment suppose that this must be. It will be the result of your fidelity to conscience which is, it can scarcely be doubted, the very voice of God within you.

In anticipation of your going to Vienna I have written to the Reverend Mr Jackson of the B. and F. Bible Society and obtained from him an introduction for you to Mr Millard of that city, the society's agent there and I only hope you may find him as kind as Mr Davies has been. By the way I have written to the latter thanking him. Probably he may, or someone else in Berlin may, give you introductions to some German family there – in Vienna.

I went to a meeting this afternoon of the directors of the London Missionary Society and tomorrow expect to attend a meeting of the sub-committee of the Congregational Union of E. and W. on church finance at the New House, the Memorial Hall in Faringdon Street.

We leave here (D.V.) on Wednesday morning, arriving at Brussels at 5.15 pm. We go through Cologne and hope to see Mary and Mima on Friday. It is very cold, as it appears by the papers to be the case with you. I hope you will be particularly careful in taking precautions against cold and rheumatism.

. . . We left all well at Wolverhampton unless we except poor Fraser and your great uncle Martin who feels his age and John Lee who does the same.

It does not seem very satisfactory to leave home with only your Uncle Harper in charge, who certainly seems slow to learn his new business. But I trust we shall be brought safely through this . . .

Now goodbye, kind remembrances to Mr and Mrs Meissner and Mr Schuster and also Mr Davies. Your affectionate father, Samuel S. Mander.

Zelten 18 Berlin February 23 1875

My very dear Father,

I am sorry to have to report badly of myself this week. Last Monday and Tuesday I was somewhat unwell. On Tuesday I was bound to go to a reception at Professor Lepsius' where Mr Davies had introduced me . . . Next morning I had such a cough and headache that I remained all day in bed. In fact, since then until today I have not left the house. Unfortunately I have been out too much today, it is very cold although fine, so that in spite of being warmly wrapped up I have a regularly bad cough tonight and hoarseness. I saw a doctor this morning and he has given me medicine. Last week I only took household remedies.

Last night we celebrated Frau Vorwerk's birthday. We had six "tableaux vivants" a great deal of costume being hired. I appeared as an officer of Louis XVII's time with blue and grey uniform, white trousers, gorgeous white peruke etc. etc. We kept our costumes on all evening. The party numbered about 40. I retired at 12, dancing was maintained til 4.

I wish you all a very pleasant and successful journey . . .

With very much love to you all . . . your loving son, Theo Mander.

. . . we have two Hungarians here now who are waiting for my room. They were told I should leave middle of March and I shan't feel . . . like keeping them out long over the time. I thought of going about the 21st . . .

Mr Schuster has gone now, I suppose on the way to Egypt. Should I give Meissner and Co. anything on leaving?

My foot has been hurting me rather, have had rheumatism in several parts.

Wednesday – in bed, headache, toothache, rheumatism are gone, only the cough remains which I hope soon to cure. One feels the difference from home food when poorly. Hope to be about my work next time I write. Please write soon, have not heard this week from home.

Diary

February 25th Thursday
My 22nd birthday. Abundance of letters from home Papa, Mama, Mary, Mima,

Nellie, Lottie will meet tomorrow D.V. in Wiesbaden; Nellie and Lot going to school in Vevey; Mary going to Versailles, Mima remaining in Wiesbaden.

I can look up with joy, and praise God for all his love during the past year. It has been a happy year. I devote myself today afresh to His service . . .

Vienna June 10 1875
My dear Father,

Just a line or two, no time for more. Mama's letter received this morning, glad to have it. Our business here is nearly accomplished[35], just been writing out special letter for Beck, Koller and Co. connected with agreement. We took stock yesterday and went to custom house today. All to be finished, including signing of agreements, here this afternoon.

Hope to start for Pesch. early tomorrow morning, by steamer on the Danube. Then back here, then Prague and Leipsic. Heard Strauss play and conduct his band last night.

. . . in a hurry. Ever your affectionate son, Theo Mander.

In 1876 Theodore spent part of the year at Cambridge University

Clare College, Cambridge May 26 1876
My dear Father,

. . . Yesterday the May boat races were concluded by a procession of about 25 eighters along the backs in their final order. They were gaudily decorated with flowers. They finally formed in close order side by side across the river, then all the crews stood up and raised their oars aloft, giving three cheers for each crew. This is the annual ceremony and certainly is a very pretty sight as all the men are dressed in their college colours, and what with coloured costumes, coloured oars and flowers, an effect of rainbow brilliancy was produced . . . Visitors will have left Cambridge in a few days altogether and men are preparing for their May exams . . . I bicycled over with Lee the other day to Fenstanton, 10 miles and paid a visit to the Cootes. We remained (for) dinner and got back about 9.30.

Weather here wet or at any rate what an Irishman would call "soft."

Hoping to be home in about ten days, with much love to all. Ever your very affectionate son, Theo Mander.

Cambridge. October 29 1876

My dear Father,

I feel I have sent you but scanty information lately concerning myself and I must now supplement my post cards with a letter.

After a tolerably active Sunday . . . I commenced my exam in tolerable spirits on Monday morning. The four subsequent days (including Monday) were similarly occupied . . . I satisfied myself in Classics, Greek History, Physiology and perhaps Moral Philosophy, but in Mathematics and Logic I was weak. They were nasty papers different from what I had expected. However I felt I'd worked conscientiously in preparing for the exam. I also felt the influence of a greater presence than my own during the exam and knew that I was not alone. Consequently I believe that the result, whatever it is, will be right. I shall know my fate at the end of this week and will communicate it to you at once.

Respecting the next six weeks, I told our tutor Mr Raynes the other day that I shall not be stopping here for my three years, indeed I might not even . . . remain to the end of this term. He asked me to get to know as soon as I could what I intended to do . . .

To tell the truth, after working almost incessantly for nearly a year I don't feel at all inclined to take it up again. Whether I have passed in London or not I do not feel sufficient energy to go on working . . . I am thoroughly sick of examinations and feel that at my age, working at such trifling subjects and learning up what I knew years ago and have forgotten is simply so much time wasted.

I should feel very thankful to have a week or two's rest, for my London preparation has both occupied my general time and filled up all leisure too, for the past few months . . . I sincerely hope I have passed in London but if I have not, I shall feel still less inclination to remain up here slaving at elementary trigonometry, algebra etc. again.

Don't you think I'd better come down shortly? I'm anxious to get to business and moreover that has more claims on me than anything else . . . I have thought the matter over carefully and really believe this would be the best course.

My stay here will have been of great value I believe, both socially and as a preparation for London and therefore (the) idea of sending me up here will by no means have been frustrated.

Please let me know in a few days what you think of this.

. . . ever your affectionate son, S. Theo Mander.

University of London, Burlington Gardens W
Sir,

I am pleased to inform you that you have passed in the First Division
I am sir, yours obediently, J. Howell. Hall Porter.

Telegram handed in by Theodore at 12.53 November 4th 1876 Cambridge

Unless the London University Hall Porter has made an error I have passed in the first class.

DIARY

December 31st Sunday
Retrospect of the past year as usual brings mingled joy and sorrow, gratitude and regret.

My whole varsity life included in the past twelve months. Spent Lent and May terms and a portion of the Winter term in Cambridge. During Long Vac spent a profitable month with a reading party of Oxford men . . . in the Lakes. Worked for final B.A. all the Vac. Was divinely assisted in this preparation and most clearly so in the exam week in October . . . Have had a very profitable year at Cambridge which I shall never regret and which I believe will be of much assistance to me in life.

Have now finally settled down to business where I have been about a month.

Sin has tarnished the brightness of the year from which and its consequences God deliver me!

. . . The foundations of my religion have been broadened, and thus I believe strengthened. I see more clearly how the essence of Christ's religion consists of love, unselfishness, sympathy and a gentle attentiveness to happiness of others in small things as well as large . . .

. . . I think we should avoid that narrow aesthetic (sic) mode of living which many tend to and fall into and rather show how our Christianity makes our sympathies wider and more lively . . .

My dear father and sister Mary are now on a tour in the East. They have visited Palestine and Egypt and we hope soon to see them home again.

February 5 1877
Dear father and Mary have returned today from the Orient, both of them benefited in health by the tour.

February 25th Sunday
My birthday. I am 24. Years are creeping on me fast and I don't seem to

accomplish much. God has been very merciful to me this past year. I have much to mourn and much to be grateful for. It's Sunday evening, my father and mother and Martin are at the Wood chapel. Mary in the drawing room, Mima in London, Nellie in Menton, Lottie in Malvern, Howard at school (T.P.S.)

I have spent a short time, for I could never pray at great length like the old saints, in strengthening prayer.

In August 1877 Theodore visited America and Canada with Howard who was 15.

The surviving holiday notes begin, on the first page of his notebook, in the middle of this holiday at Niagara falls.

Continuation of American Trip

August 22

Rose and threw open my wooden venetians and walked out on the verandah, when one of the finest natural panoramas suddenly burst on my view. The sun had risen, but was not hot enough to dispel the veil of mist that hung before the Falls. The soft fleecy vapours were gradually lifting from the river while behind them shone the glittering walls, decking the long ridge of precipice with purest white . . . Over all the fresh young sun cast golden floods of light.

I think I never witnessed so glorious a scene.

After breakfast we took the cars to Niagara town where we went on board the steamer for Toronto.

The lake was a great still sheet of blue on which the sun shone brilliantly . . . Toronto rose in the distance, before losing sight of the opposite shore, very like Dover with white cliffs on either side . . . Then inside the long natural breakwater formed by Gibraltar Point, and came up alongside the quay.

Took a room at the Queen's . . .

Rambled through the town. A prosperous and cleanly place, though not as showy as many American cities . . .

Went through College Avenue to the Toronto University, the only one I believe in Canada. A fine building in nearly pure Norman style. Numerous good lecture rooms. Large convocation Hall for examinations. Laboratory, Capital Museum and a Library which I did not see. Cosy rooms fitted up in a similar manner to rooms at Cambridge.

About 300 attend the University, 50 living in the building, the others living out. Nearly all Canadians, only about a dozen or so Americans. 4 years course. Residence not essential. Various denominational Colleges prepare for the University which is quite un-sectarian. There is no chapel in the building, each man attending the church of his own denomination in the city.

Ground in front for Sports Park and plenty of trees around. (Queen's Park)

August 23 Sunday
Attended service at the Cathedral, a fine large structure of Gothic architecture built of Portland stone etc. Is surmounted by highest tower on the continent, made of iron . . .

Walked out 2 miles to the very extensive brick-built lunatic asylum. 50 acres of ground attached, and laid out with trees and walks for the benefit of the inmates who number about 700. Could not visit interior . . .

24th
Left Toronto 7 am. Arrived Belleville 12 am. Fertile country all along, mostly under cultivation. In one place however train stopped where nothing was visible but the forest and the small wooden station. Little rising towns border the lake. Spent 12 hours in Belleville with Mr Graham. Discussed varnishes and the trade. Drove round the town and neighbourhood. 10,000 pop. very active and rising – along a long bay extending right away to Kingston. Plenty of yachting. Went over the deaf and dumb institution for Province of Ontario.

245 inmates, all children. Saw boys learning trades, carpentering and shoe making and girls working.

Handsome Town Hall with clock tower. Good market.

Train to Kingston at midnight.

September 25
Left Kingston per steamer at 6 am.

Slept for a couple of hours and woke to find ourselves in the middle of the far-famed Thousand Islands through which we steamed for an hour or two.

The river is so wide and the islands so low that the general effect fell rather short of my preconceived ideas. However . . . The islands are multitudinous and of all shapes and sizes and this combined with the incipient autumnal tints of the foliage and the bright day, added a great charm to the journey . . . Two insignificant rapids form the advance guard by two or three hours of the great attractions of the river.

About 4, after passing Prescott, we ascertained ahead the breakers of the first genuine rapids.

The current increases in rapidity, and swirls round in whirlpools and backwards in curling waves; it boils and bubbles and seethes as if over a terrific subterranean fire. Rocks rarely protrude above the surface, but one can often detect them just through the water. We passed amongst others, the Long Sault . . . and Split Rock Rapids, at the last passing between . . . ledges not more than 40 ft. apart . . . The velocity is very great, being in one place as much as 30 miles an hour . . . the effect of the immense speed round the curves is often to raise one portion of the water, generally the outer, a foot or two above another.

The last rapids, called Lachine, we were obliged to omit, for the darkness at this season coming on so early, the steamer traverses the canal made to avoid the rapids for vessels passing up.

. . . a large thunderstorm commenced which lasted 2-3 hours and proved the finest I had ever seen. Every variety of lightning occurred. Yellow and pink sheet lightning, some gentle and distant, some in the immediate atmosphere and intensely bright . . . Thunder was intermittent . . . The rain poured in torrents for a short time, and in black darkness relieved only by this . . . light we traversed the Lachine canal and reached Montreal about 8 pm . . .

September 26

Perambulated Montreal . . .

Entered the R.C. Cathedral . . . a very large white stone building with two towers, 240 ft high, very like N.D. in Paris. This church is however plainer outside but excessively gaudy inside, being bedaubed freely in every part with red, blue and yellow . . . Will seat 7-8,000.

. . . there are many fine stores and the general appearance of the city from an elevation is very grand.

Many domes and towers, abundance of trees, and Mont Royal, well wooded, rises behind, with the great river, its islands and stupendous bridge in front.

Wandered about the fine quays and docks and surveyed the variety of vessels lying there. Noticed many from England . . .

Through the beautiful grounds attached to the McGills College and University. Moderate sized and not very handsome building. About 3-400 students. Excellent medical degree . . . Saw . . . fine collections of scientific instruments and models, very good. Museum of Shells and comfortable library of 30,000 vols. Course 3-4 years . . .

Train for Ottawa 10 pm.

September 27

Rolled through a fertile region, mostly cultivated but still retaining patches of forest. Glided gently in the moonlight over the level plain and across rivers as far as Prescott where our Pullman car was detached and waited 4 hours, after which it was attached afresh and we pursued our journey in the early dawn to Ottawa.

Slept well in the car and arrived refreshed to breakfast at the Russell House.

Visited the Parliament House and Departmental buildings.

These are very extensive and handsome buildings and strike one very pleasingly as they suddenly burst on one's sight on turning the corner of some street. They occupy the three sides of a large quadrangle which is laid with turf and they stand on a conspicuous eminence overlooking both town and river. The style is Gothic with narrow and sharp pointed windows . . . A number of towers and pinnacles give the whole a very elegant appearance.

House of Commons is an elegant well appointed chamber, arranged so that the 260 members sit on opposite sides according to their politics. Dark wood, light from above, gaslight from reflecting gaseliers in the ceiling.

Senate Chamber . . .

Supreme Court of Justice . . . Visited the infernal hells whence blasts of hot and cold air alternately warm and ventilate the rooms and passages above.

Library of the House is a charmingly complete and elegant octagonal building full of books and tastefully ornamented with deal wood fittings.

. . . Visited *St Patricks* a plain and large R.C. Cathedral.

A *Normal School* well supplied with large lecture rooms . . . etc. Everything clean, airy and attractive . . .

Ottawa has more fine public buildings for its size than any town I know.

Splendid Post Office and Court House and City Hall . . . The place swarms with Scotchmen.

. . . Entered a lumber mill, and saw the trees after being barked and lying 1-4 years in the river hauled up an incline plane into the building, where they are at once sawn by steam power into about 1 doz. planks, about 5 mins. sufficing to despatch a tree of 12 ft. The planks are then placed on a bench where a revolving chain with occasional pegs drags them through another saw that takes their rough edges off. Hence they are removed to be piled up and allowed to season about a year. A tree worth 50 cents – 1 dollar. A sawn plank 16 ft. by 12 ins by 2 ins worth about 30 cents. Walked beyond the edge of the town into the woods by the river, and enjoyed one of the loveliest scenes in nature . . .

Forest stretching away into the misty distance. The lumber filled river glimmering away far back into the cheery sunlight; and a fresh invigorating air whetting ones appetite for real enjoyment of the landscape.

Took horse-car 3 miles to other end of the city limits. Saw there the rocky ledge onto which the Rideau Falls usually tumble. The waters happened to be turned in another channel when we were there.

Walked through the wooded grounds to Lord Dufferin's[36] comfortable but not imposing residence. Were refused admission by soldier-janitor. Family at home, though His Excellency and the Countess are on a visit to Manitoba, exploring the Red River and haranguing the inhabitants of Winnipeg.

September 28

Six o'clock in the morning and a cloudy sky with a fresh cold wind. Such is our outlook as we hastily dress and collect our scanty baggage for a return trip on the Ottawa river to Montreal. A large 'bus, probably licensed for twenty takes ourselves and one other aboard as its entire cargo and carries us at a swinging pace to the wharf.

Here lies the steamer "Peerless" a broad and handsome river boat, with capacity for perhaps 200 passengers. After due deliberation for reception of a score of persons and their baggage, our engine employs its pent up energies, the great paddle-wheels revolve and we push away from shore, launched on the peaceful bosom of the broad but shallow river.

We are not on the Mississippi so don't fear snags. We are not navigating the Thames and are not expectant of collision. Nor yet do we float on the treacherous Amazon, and therefore have no dread of crocodiles. In fact this is not likely to prove a very eventful voyage . . .

The leaden sky does not deceive us, but soon begins to descend and wrap the earth in its clammy arms. From the warm snug cabin we can survey the landscape in comfort, and dry clothes. However we first despatch a hot and hearty breakfast, ensconce ourselves on the cushioned seats and divide our attention between the excitements of fiction and the peaceful attractions of the world without. Beneath us the broad river flows undisturbed except by pattering raindrops. On either side are rich fringes of forest land made gaudy with all the varied and vivid tints of a Canadian fall. Here a sombre brown decks a fading beech, there a brilliant flash of crimson lights up the general modesty of foliage; somewhere the original green still lives in all its variety of shade and hue, but the general colour that pervades the whole is a mellow orange or delicate lemon yellow. From time to time a clearing in the woods is noticeable, where some industrious and enterprising woodsman is labouring to reclaim the land from its primeval wildness and bring it under the gentler influences of cultivation.

Occasionally a group of fields already ploughed may be seen and near them a tiny village of rude timber huts.

But there are few, and the land yet offers boundless advantages to the pioneering settler, and promises to repay his honest efforts with ample reward.

So the scenery goes on, the monotony of beauty almost palling on the mind which is too coarse to fully appreciate it.

Here one page has been torn out but the account of the river journey continues later the same day on the following page

Owing to rapids we took train. A most primitive affair. Grass grown road . . . on which the shaky carriages roll as if on the swelling waves.

Steamboat again; the river broadens and twice expands in a lake. At Lachine we take the cars again for Montreal to avoid the great rapids.

Arrived 6 pm.

Supper then a rummage through the dark streets.

September 29
Went Skin-hunting and laid in a stock fit to rig out a Siberian family for the winter.

. . . Sought admittance to the Grey Nunnery, but were refused by a curt spoken sister, who explained after much pumping that they were cleaning.

Watched a portion of a Lacrosse match between two strong teams, the Toronto and Montreal. Saw two goals won by the former.

Drove round the Mont Royal, a lovely little excursion . . .

Visited the charmingly wooded English cemetery behind the hill. Quite a garden of nature, full of winding avenues and brilliant with autumn tints.

. . . Dined, packed and went aboard the steamer "Montreal" for Quebec at 7 pm. Dark starlight night.

Moon rose about 9, a thick orange crescent, reflecting a rich refulgence in the water . . .

Faint streaks of the Northern Lights strike upwards as I chat with an old countryman, settled out here, of hard winters, sport, commerce, society etc.

Bed at 11.

30th Sunday
Wake and rise at 6.30 to find that instead of Quebec, it is only the village of Batiscan where we lie motionless, having been stopped at 2 am by the dense fog. Shortly however the sun appears, disperses the fog which rolls away in clouds (bell tolls for matins as we leave) and we continue our journey between shores like parti-coloured fringes passing numerous villages of brilliant white wooden cottages, white even to the wood-tiled roof.

Reach Quebec at 12 am. Fine appearance of city from the river.

Scaled the heights in the flimsiest of old vehicles (caleche) resembling a big armchair on wheels.

Lunched at St Louis Hotel.

. . . Visited the extensive citadel; an Irish soldier conducted us over the immense and strong fortifications, and pointed out the spots where Wolfe and Montgomery respectively fell.

The view from these Heights of Abraham is surprisingly grand, probably one of the finest in the world. First the quaint old town sloping down with all its variously shaped and coloured buildings, 200 ft to the river, the latter covered with numerous shipping including some very large craft. Beyond, Point Levi with its scattered houses and churches and forts. On the left a straggling village stretched out to Montmorenci (sic) Falls and beyond is the great range of mountains extending from Labrador to the Rocky Mountains.

Walked the exceedingly ill-kept Governor's Gardens a public promenade. Wandered through the narrow and dusty and steep streets and alleys and stairs of the city and noted the nearly universal French . . .

October 1

Took a stylish looking carriage and pair and drove nine miles through the long straggling village of Beauport to the Falls of Montmerenci. Fine views of Quebec on the way. Houses nearly all wooden with wood tiles, and a ladder permanently resting on the roof to be used in case of fire. Double doors and windows showed how great the cold is in winter. Pop. entirely French.

Owing to the prevalence of the old French laws respecting land, the farms become divided up into very small portions, and the cultivation of the soil consequently very much impeded. These French Canadians also do not strike out from the beaten track; they do nothing towards settling the interior and don't even cultivate well the coastline which they inhabit.

Passed some pretty old-fashioned residences nestling amongst ruddy and mellow foliage.

The Falls have a height of 200 ft sheer. There was but little water at the time of our visit, but . . . the effect must be impressive when water abounds . . .

On our return we called at the extensive Lunatic Asylum for Province of Quebec. 900 inmates. 500 female. 400 male . . .

Very neat and clean.

The women were all indoors and were scattered thickly through the sitting rooms, some lying flat on the seats, some sitting and swaying backwards and forwards . . . some singing . . .

One woman sat outside with a large gilt crown on and other decorations, believing herself a Queen.

The men were also indoors . . . all looking very degraded except one who shook hands and explained to us that his name was "Dr. Saint Simon Peter Munger, Elijah the Prophet, the Second Moses, the new law giver unto Eternal Life, Jesus Christ the second, the Holy Ghost, the Comforter, the Rock of God of Ages."

He had preached the Kingdom of God throughout Canada , and believed he was known throughout the world, even in China and Japan. Said he was placed in here for jealousy and was now preaching to the souls in hell. When he came out and formed his kingdom and gathered his 10,000 virgins, then Heaven would commence on earth. Sent a message by us to Queen Victoria asking her to come and be his wife and reign with him.

All this was said in a perfectly serious manner and with a natural voice. He is 70 years old, has been confined 10 years and has a long beard and hair all flowing down together.

Drove to the Plains of Abraham, saw the ancient battle-field, and the monument where Wolfe fell, a simple obelisk crowned with a helmet and sword.

Passed . . . the Market, the new Rink, the new Parliament Buildings now rising.

Drove along the Battery a terrace armed with cannon. Saw the thick walls which surround the city.

Went over the present Parliament Building . . .

In the evening went to hear the Bishop describe his late visit to Labrador. Unfortunately the audience was small, owing to a heavy thunderstorm, so his Lordship was persuaded to postpone his lecture. A Rev. Mr Appleton described his missionary labours north of Lake Superior. 14,000 whites and 16,000 Indians in the diocese, which was that of Algoma. He reckoned 6,000 Indians only, were actually heathen.

October 2

Left Quebec by the "St Lawrence" a fine river steam-boat with comfortable saloon, well heated with stoves and supplied with a profusion of easy-chairs and sofas. Started at 8 am.

Steamed away east . . . Passed Isle d'Orleans . . . Then Gros Isle comes in sight, the Quarantine of the river.

Now the river obtains enormous breadth. We coast close along the northern side which all along is most brilliantly decked with coloured foliage, covering the mountains to their very tops . . . The peculiar characteristic here, which lends a special charm to the colouring, is the general intermixture of the darkest pines, relieving the gaudiness of the splendid panorama . . .

First calling place is Baie St Paul between Isle aux Coudres and the coast. A secluded little village exposing but a few cottages to view . . .

Then Murray Bay, across to Riviere-du-Loup, and back to Tadousac (sic) all of which are favourite watering-places and much revisited too in summer by the Montrealers and Quebecers . . .

Tadousac lies at the mouth of the Saguenay and we approach it in the dark, at about 9 pm . . .

A great source of interest for travellers by the boat, is found in the hurry and bustle that ensues on the arrival at any of the stations en route. After firmly securing the vessel by ropes, planks are swiftly thrown out and form a strong causeway to the wooden piers.

Then a constant ebb and flow of passengers, and especially of goods, sets in. Barrels of flour, fish, soap etc. miscellaneous articles of merchandise such as iron bars and plates, bedsteads, carriages and occasionally a horse, are moved swiftly backwards and forwards for 5 to 10 minutes, then the bell rings and off we go again.

October 3

Rose at 6 to find our vessel lying in Ha! Ha! Bay. Walked round the village . . .

Very struggling place. Awfully remote and lonesome . . .

Proceeded further up the river to Chicoutimi. Similar place but rather larger. Extensive seminary for children's education conducted by the priests, also an immense church building.

Sailed back to mouth of Saguenay River, Chicoutimi to Tadousac, about 12-6 pm. Finest part about the middle where Cape Eternity rises 1800 ft from the water, very precipitous and black . . .

About 9 years ago, 90 miles of the river was visited with a destructive fire in the forests. We saw here and there masses of dead trees still standing.

Landed at Tadousac, the favourite watering place of Lord Dufferin where he has built a summer residence.

Cross the St Lawrence, here 20 miles wide, and land at Riviere-du-Loup about 8 pm.

Primitive spring vehicle conveys us through 3 dark miles to La Rochelle Hotel.

October 4

Riviere-du-Loup

Prices through whole Canada [37]

Beef (best)	7 cents per 1 lb highest
Mutton	6 cents per 1 lb
Pork	5 – 8 cents per 1 lb
Potatoes	20 cents per bushel
Turnips	(ditto)
Oats	30 – 40 cents per bushel
Wheat best	1½ – 2 dollars per bushel
Salmon	5 – 9 cents per 1 lb
Wheat in Upper Canada	75 cents per bushel
Flour best	5 – 6 dollars per barrel of 200 lbs
Wages :-	
Labourer	60 cents – 1½ dollars per day
Bricklayer	Winter 2 dollars, Summer 2 ½ dollars
Carpenter	1½ dollars per day
Good wooden house for labourer finished and furnished	300 – 350 dollars.

After suffering a breakdown in a bug-board or spring-board vehicle, we reached the station in a villainous spring-less cart, seated on our luggage. At 12.30 we left . . . for St John New Brunswick.

Travelled 18 hours through a wild inhospitable country, consisting mostly of untouched forests . . . Very little human habitation, the train sometimes stopping where nothing but the wooden station was in sight . . .

October 5

Arrived St John N.B. at 6 am and put up at the infamous Waverley Hotel which is about the best left after the fire.

Called on Arthur Tippet[38] at 8.30 and found him after a day's acquaintance a first rate fellow. He drove us through the city which is beautifully situated on several hills, and is singularly difficult to understand on account of the varying elevation of the ground and the winding of the St John River. It rained heavily nearly all day and was in fact, the first wet day we had had, so we could not possibly complain.

The city largely consists of disreputable looking wooden buildings, and the streets are hopelessly muddy and uneven. There are however some pretty private residences and a number of fine brick and stone buildings are now rising in the heart of the city. We witnessed some of the ravages of the terrible fire of June last but already 700 buildings are going up, and soon all traces of the disaster will have been effaced.

The staple trade of the city is lumber, and the quays are quite busy with shipping.

Visited the fine large rink where the Relief Committee is now located. Its work is done very systematically and efficiently, being organised by a gentleman from Chicago who discharged a similar service to Chicago after its great conflagration.

The YMCA has a very good structure, but I hear it has rather degenerated into a rendezvous for working men and shop girls and even worse characters.

. . . Spent a pleasant evening with Arthur Tippet and his brother at their lodgings

October 6

Yesterday a heavy gale had been blowing and had kept back the Boston steam boat more than 16 hours . . . The wind had now subsided and the sun shone out brightly. So we embarked on the steam boat "Empress" at 8 am and crossed the Bay of Fundy, where fogs usually reign supreme . . . Crossed over in about 4 hours to Digby and then steamer up an inland basin to Annapolis, arriving there at 2 pm.

Here we took cars at 3 and traversed the beautiful valley that runs along the northern coast of Nova Scotia from the above town to Windsor.

Near the south of Annapolis River a great deal of land has been reclaimed and is preserved by dykes . . .

We took in quite a crowd of respectable, well dressed, strong and healthy looking excursionists at Kentville where the Provincial fair was being held. Changed at Windsor where we had checked our baggage to, and forgot to have it rechecked. Consequently we arrived about 10.30 pm at Halifax without any baggage and after finding the quiet and select Waverley Hotel quite full, put up at the "Halifax" a large but not very clean commercial house.

On the way from Windsor, a man said to be drunk, fell off the train and we had to return some distance for him. He was found bruised and wounded and, said one authority, lying to his waist in water.

After duly mourning the loss of our luggage we retired to bed, with the determination to spend the next day in seclusion.

October 7
Decked out in the dingy attire of travellers we slunk into a neighbouring Baptist chapel some time after the commencement of service.

To my utter astonishment and to the disturbance of my subsequent devotions my eyes suddenly rested on Flora sitting in a side pew directly under the minister, apparently with her mother, father and brother. Immediately the service concluded we bolted . . .

PM Had prayer together and wrote letters and notes . . . Baptist chapel again at night, after a good walk.

October 8
While breakfasting at the hotel, Mr Paint and Flora called. Went with them shopping etc.

At midday we went to Mr Paint's and put up there, leaving the hotel.

Fetched luggage in the evening from station.

October 9
Crossed harbour by ferry. Took "one-hoss-shay" and drove ourselves (Flora, Madmoiselle Hugerenin, Arthur, Howard and myself) to the gold diggings of Waverley, 10 miles from Halifax.

No work was going on at the time but we had the whole process described to us.

Mining the quartz in shafts, 2-300 ft deep, with lateral galleries.

Crushing with hammers in water. Dust washed through a sieve (400 to an inch) Gold amalgamates with mercury mixed with the crushed ore. The whole adheres to copper plates, where it is scamped. The Hg. then is distilled off, leaving the pure gold in the iron crucible . . .

Many diggings here now abandoned.

Returned and spent a very cosy afternoon and evening singing etc.

The remaining entries in this notebook were written in French

October 10
In the evening everyone went to a prayer meeting, everyone except Flora and myself. We passed the time in the house and something very important and agreeable occurred . . .

Flora 1877

October 11-12-13th
We amused ourselves wonderfully, by car, on foot, in the town and in our friends' house, there with the family, M. et Madame Paint, Flora, Arthur, Mademoiselle Hugerenin, a Swiss lady, Howard and myself.

October 14 Sunday
Flora and I went to the Baptist church in the morning and were exposed to the curious gaze of a whole crowd of people. We felt very proud and happy . . .

October 15
I went shopping in the town in the morning and in the afternoon, after packing . . . I spent several hours of sheer joy with my darling!!

October 16
We went on board the steamer "Caspian" accompanied by M. Paint, Flora, and Arthur. After waiting half an hour and making our farewells, the boat cast off and sailed into the bay. Everyone waved their handkerchiefs without crying, even though we felt like it just the same.

We found ourselves en route to the high seas. Little by little the last rocks of the great port of Halifax disappeared over the horizon and for several hours we skirted the wild and picturesque coast of Nova Scotia.

After eating . . . I went to my cabin and at last fell asleep.

October 17
In bed feeling unwell

October 18
Arriving at St Johns, Newfoundland, Howard and I visited the strange town . . . The Episcopal church is a rather beautiful building inside. It has an air of English comfort. The Catholic church is large and simply decorated in blue and white . . .

We stopped for two hours while the trunks and merchandise were taken on and off. We left this inhospitable climate in fog which meant we could not see the coast further than a mile. The wind was quite strong and the vessel was being prepared for a storm.

October 19
I stayed in bed because of sea sickness, which attacked me only once.

October 20
Little wind, no rain. I got up.

October 21
. . . prayers this morning with a congregation of over a dozen . . . Fine weather.

October 22
Fine weather all the time with a light following wind. The sea was high with enormous waves . . . carrying us every day nearer our destination.

The detailed notes about his holiday end here but he continued to list dates, and numbers recording the distance between Halifax and Liverpool, where they arrived on October 25th

322 Grays Inn Road, London. October 29th 1877
My very dear Theodore,

I was glad beyond measure to get your letter this morning, its contents rejoiced me *immensely*. Of course you know well that news of such an event could not be surprising to me! In fact it seems to me the most natural thing in the world and quite the *best thing*! I always felt that there was but one thing wanting to make Flora a really splendid girl and now that she has the one thing needful I believe she is worth her weight in gold . . . I really do think that she is more suited to you than anyone else I have known, and as for myself I'm delighted . . . she is worthy of you and you of her I think. How happy you must be! and how thankful we must all be to God that He has so answered our prayers and thus made this event possible!

. . . I . . . have already added her photo to those of our family on my dressing table. I think it is her proper place though perhaps you would think it too public.

I was glad of what you said at the end of your letter about your love to us. I shall always remember those words and trust them.

With best love, ever your affectionate sister Mima.

The Mount October 30th 1877
My dearest Theodore,

Very many thanks for troubling to send me the gloves. It was very good of you to remember them, they are lovely ones . . .

Why did you not tell me you were engaged to Flora Paint? I longed to ask you on Saturday if you were but thought perhaps you would not like me to. I am so glad Theodore. I long to see you to give you my congratulations. Flora Paint was such a nice jolly girl, I liked her very much. What fun to think of her as being your wife very very soon. I wish you every happiness . . . With much love, believe me dear Theodore,

Yours very affectionately, A. Julia Mander.

Drumgawe November 7th 1877
My dearest Flora,

I was rather surprised to see the familiar handwriting this morning and my joy knew no bounds when I saw what the letter contained. My dear Flora, I wish you *all* happiness and all the rest of it, in this affecting time.

I do hope you are coming to live on this side of the pond, and if any time you and Mr Mander should come to Bonnie Scotland do not forget to let me know.

Unaccustomed as I am to write notes of this description to my friends in general, I hope you will excuse all deficiencies and remember that "the flesh is willing though the spirit is weak." Spirit refers to mind and that sort of arrangement.

If you could send me a photo of the happy man I should be so glad, as from your description he must be nothing short of an Adonis, and I should like to feel that my conjecture is right.

As I wrote you yesterday I shall not lengthen out this epistle, so wishing you all happiness which I am sure you will have,

Believe me, Your loving friend, Annie Sempleton

Holiday notebook

American trip commenced June 21/78 Mima and myself
Received at starting (inc. $10 previously)

	Cash	$90
	Cheques – 2	$40
Expended :-		
June 21	Return tickets (2) Liverpool to N.Y.	$63
	Wolverhampton to Liverpool	$1
June 21	Reached Liverpool and visited Edith and Grendon[39] at Rockferry.	
June 22	3 pm. Sailed out of the Mersey on board SS "Skythier" Weather fine.	
June 23	Sunday	

Moored in Queenstown harbour. Mima and I went ashore. Attended very profitable service at Protestant Church of Ireland.

Visited Royal Sailors' Home and found it in excellent order. Two or three of its inmates had just come in from a vessel bound for the Cape and now lying in harbour. It leaked, they saw, 3 ft. per hour and Captain and crew refused to go further. Owners intended to obtain fresh captain and crew at 20/- per month extra and send the ship on without repairs!

June 24
In berth all day. Sky dull, sea leaden . . .

26th
Sea moderate. Rose at midday.

While sea was running under a heavy swell, sudden cry of "man overboard" Steerage passenger, under 30, threw himself over while suffering from D.T.'s Engines stopped, boat lowered with 4 men and 4th. officer, rowed to scene of disaster, picked up life-buoy, saw no trace of the man. Boat disappeared from time to time altogether from view in trough of the sea.

Hauled her in again and proceeded.

This occurred at dinner hour, 6 pm, and seemed to make little impression on the passengers . . .

29th
Sea quite calm. Bright sun. Warm.

Passed through a shoal of whales, which we saw rolling and spouting by the dozen.

11.30 pm Songs and stories in the smoke room, with much boisterous merriment. Mr de Cordova master of ceremonies.

12 pm Discerned a ship's lights at some distance and fired rockets but obtained no answer. Clear starlight. No moon.

30th Sunday
Sea very calm. Warm. No service as tonight captain was detained on bridge by fog. Passed through shoal of porpoises. They leaped clear out of the water in direction of ship, apparently trying to keep up. Reminded one very much of street boys turning wheel somersaults by a carriage.

We remained all day even with a German steamer from Hamburg, 2-3 miles.

July 1 Monday
Sea calm. Weather warm. Bright sun. Frequent fogs.

Notes of passengers:-

Discussion between de Cordova, Mr Harper and a professor re. religion.

De C. announced himself an utter sceptic. No Bible, no atonement, no Trinity, no immortality . . . Believed sin brought its own reward inevitably . . . Said men made their own God in all ages; men had taken a glass and cast a magnified image of themselves into space and called that God.

Harper defended Christian religion . . .

When de C. alluded to the Trinity, Prof. said "D . . . the Trinity!"

Rev. Parker, Catholic priest, sort of Falstaff, jolly fellow. Sang low love songs, sprinkled with oaths on Sunday afternoon. Had no service for the Irish Catholic on board who told their beads all to themselves. Spent his time smoking, did not hesitate to use profane language and quote Scripture and defend the Mass etc. with all levity.

Gentleman, wife, daughter and little son of about 6 years from Frisco, been in Europe some months. He went over from Scotland 30 years ago. Walked on foot from St Louis across the plains.

Numerous visitors returning from Paris exhibition. About 90% of the passengers are American.

Carouse in smoke room.

July 2 Tuesday
Midnight of the 1st, stopped and sounded owing to the thick fog which prevailed. Found 32 fathoms which was right for Nantucket shoals. Kept on our course and hailed a fishing boat mistaken in the fog for a pilot. Soon after, picked up pilot No. 20, who bought newspapers to 27th ult.

Rose at 4.15. Fog had cleared but sky was completely shrouded. Clouds soon rolled away and permitted a fine sunrise like a clean cut molten ball over a cloud bank lying close on the horizon.

Took a bath of sea water.

6 am. Sky clear and bright, air warm. Entered N.Y. harbour in hot and brilliant weather.

Passed the custom officers speedily by dint of much running about.

Took a companion with us in a carriage, and after driving a keen bargain, paid 5 dollars 50 cents for ourselves and luggage to Fifth Avenue Hotel!

July 3

Visited Stewarts' retail store . . . Roof of Equitable Life Insurance Building and splendid office of the Company inside . . . Wall Street, Kennedy House, . . . Delmonico's.

Overhead railway from Trinity Church to 23rd. Street for 5th. Ave. It is light and airy, steady and elegantly got up, but a great disfigurement to the street. Runs from the Battery to Central Park up 6th Ave. etc.

Trinity Church is a most elegant structure especially inside. Brown sandstone with dark wooden roof and dark oak seats and fittings. Fine stained glass windows. The whole blends most harmoniously in excellent taste, rich yet simple.

Saw Stewarts' Marble Palace. All windows closed with white blinds with a broad gold stripe round and near the edges, these set off the white marble wonderfully and produced a most chaste and charming effect.

Drove round Central Park six miles. Thousands of glow-worms or fireflies and a few mosquitoes.

July 4

Accompanied Mr Gifford to his house in Newark.

Stayed overnight there. Made acquaintance of Mrs G. and Charlie their son, also of Mr and Mrs Dennis. Received much hospitality from both families. Was driven out behind Mr D's Essex a quiet trotter and another horse. Sat out late in the warm air and listened to and watched gun-firing and fireworks in celebration of Independence Day.

July 5

Drove out Mr G's Union, a pretty stallion that is said to have trotted a mile in 2 mins. 17 sec. Very hot.

Examined Charlie G's telephone and microphone . . .

Was shown over Valentine's Works in Brooklyn, with *exception of rooms for storing gum, and oil – preparing rooms* . . .

Varnish made in large open pots . . . of perhaps 50-60 galls. capacity.

Run on wheels over a grate, like our own, but under a big chimney by which fumes escape into the open air . . .

Under 50 men said to be employed on entire works.

Make all their own cans and cases . . . Barrels also made on the premises.

Machines employed for stamping tin, which is passed round the room through its several processes. One of the men told me that only the best English tin is used . . .

All consumers pay carriage outside New York city.

Visited exhibition of phonograph at offices of Phonograph Co. on Broadway. "Mary had a little lamb" etc.

Expended :- [40]

2 Fans	60c
Pair of gloves for Mima	1$.00
Appleton's guide	2$.00
2 ices at Delmonico's	50c
Carriage, ices and lemonade, Central Park	1$.20c
Horse cars, stages and overhead railway	50c
1 pint Claret	40c
Bill at Fifth Ave. Hotel	20$.00
Tickets to Newport	5$.00
Luggage	1$.00

Took boat for Newport. Sailed up Long Island Sound by moonlight. Arrived Newport 4 am.

July 6

. . . Train to Boston in afternoon.

July 7 Sunday

Trinity church with Mr Day. Fine building, richly and tastefully decorated . . .

Afternoon. Visited Mr and Mrs Briggs . . .

Evening. Attended service in lecture room of Park St. Chapel . . .

July 8

Visited State House . . . and markets.

Left at 7 pm for St John. Pullman sleeping-car.

July 9

Arrived Bangor . . . at 5 pm. Went right on, per drawing-room car to St John, arriving 7 pm. Drove round the town crossing the suspension, whence we obtained a splendid view.

Stayed at Dufferin Hotel.

July 10

Left St John at 8.30 am . . . arriving Halifax at 8 pm. Flora and Mr Paint met us.

July 10 – 22

Remained in Halifax. Visited various friends . . . Made trips to Cow Bay, Point Pleasant, round North West Arm, up the Harbour towards Bedford Basin as far as Tufts Cove.

Expended :-

Glove and handkerchief boxes for Mary P.[41]	10 dollars
Pencil case for Flora	8 dollars
Photos	75 cents
Music for Mary P.	50 cents
Shampoo	40 cents
Servants	5 dollars
2 tickets to Liverpool from Quebec	150 dollars

July 22

Left Halifax per Intercolonial Railway for Montreal.

6 pm Monday till 6 am Wednesday.

July 24

Stayed at Windsor Hotel. Best in Canada, esteemed it equal to 5th Ave. NY.

Took train for Lachine 7.15 am. Shot rapids and returned to Montreal . . . by 9.15 am. Perambulated the town . . .

Took steamboat for Quebec at 7 pm . . .

July 27 Saturday

Left Quebec at 9 am per SS "Polynesian." . . . Bright fine day.

July 28 Sunday

Very fine day. Slight west wind . . . Very hot in sun.

. . . Saw two lighthouses. Steamer "Lake Megantic" of Beaver Line, said to be ashore, did not see her but captain did . . . Run to 12 am – 338 miles.

July 29 Monday

. . . Warm morning. About midday turned suddenly cold on approaching ice.

. . . coasted along Newfoundland . . .

All coasts bleak, bare, mountainous, few trees. A lighthouse here and there and a few fishing huts and sheds for fish-drying, all painted white and very visible.

. . . During afternoon saw several icebergs, one or two large ones, apparently 75 – 100 ft above the water; not like ice, transparent, but dull and glistening like ice-cream and purest white. Saluted a barque, she ran up signals.

Saw partial eclipse of sun through smoked glass very plainly. Total along a line from Jamaica through the western States to Behring Straits.

The entries for the next five days are confined to records of temperature air pressure and mileage.

August 4 Sunday
Warm, calm and cloudy. Reached Lough Foyle about 3 pm . . . West coast of Lough dotted with pretty villas and villages nestling in little woods. Land closely cultivated. Landed mails and a few passengers and took on board pilot.

On leaving a stiff breeze blew but quietened down later in the evening. Saw Giant's Causeway in the distance.

Monday August 5
Reached Mersey bar about 10 am, came in to Princes Dock landing stage by tender at 11 am.

Safely home at 4 pm to find all in their usual health, though some away, and house looking just lovely.

Thanks be to God. S.T.M.

Received – returned by Cunard Co. for return tickets not used £18.18s.0

Spent on whole tour – £133. 6s. 0 (per day each = 30s. 4d)

The Wolverhampton Chronicle was published every Friday – the following announcement appeared in the Chronicle on June 4th., 1879.

Marriages
Mander – Paint. On the 29th. ult., at Halifax, Nova Scotia, Samuel Theodore, eldest son of Samuel S. Mander, of Tettenhall, Wolverhampton, to Flora St. Clair, eldest daughter of Henry Paint, of Halifax.

The following speech is headed by Geoffrey Mander's pencilled note "1879 – Philip Vale[42] *on STM's return from wedding trip."*

Mr Chairman and friends . . . on the present occasion . . . I must say something . . . in connection with the youthful career of the young gentleman that has favoured us with his presence here today and first of all I shall just notice a few of the visits that I have known him pay to the works during his schoolboy days with his quick sight and anxious enquiry as to what is that . . . and Philip, where does this go to and who uses the other. I just mention this to show that nothing then anymore than now seemed to escape his notice . . . I need not say how glad me and all my fellow workmen are to behold his face once more amongst us again after his journey from America . . . and I must . . . say that it gives me very great pleasure to wish to both him and his wife a long life and all the happiness that this uncertain world can afford . . . I think that I must not close my remarks without saying a word or two in reference to the young lady that now rejoices in the name of Mrs Theodore Mander . . . I think you may esteem it no small privilege to be united by marriage to a family like the Manders family . . . all that have known them . . . would . . . give their testimony to their kindness to all around them and you, I have no doubt, will be entertained at many a party, you will receive many a hearty welcome and many a wish for your happiness, but believe me none will respond more heartily to the wish for your future happiness than the work people of your honourable husband . . .

After working in the family business for three years, at the age of 26, Theodore and his cousin were appointed directors of the company.

Mr C.T. Mander and Mr S.T. Mander request the pleasure of the Company of . . . to Dinner at the Exchange on Monday the 15 inst. at 6 o'clock to celebrate their entrance into the firm of Mander Brothers. December 1st. 1879.

1880 – 1900

In 1881 the death was announced of Samuel Small Mander

Basford House, Whalley Range. Manchester November 8 1881
My dear Theo,

Your note 6th inst. intimating the removal of a well known figure from our family circle did not cause me regret. I was disposed to sing with Chas. Wesley

"Rejoice for a brother deceased
Our loss is his infinite gain."

On Thursday I hope to be in my place to show my last respects for one for whom in an intercourse of more than 40 years, I had learned to love and I believe he fully reciprocated the affection.

With kindest regards to all in your circle, believe me to remain,
Yours faithfully, Henry B. Jackson.

Extracts from Theodore Mander's notebook on the early development of his children[43]

Geoffrey le Mesurier Mander
Born March 6th 1882. 8½ lbs
Biography begun July 5th 1883
Past particulars from memory are as follows:-

Flora and Geoffrey 1882

. . . First raised himself to his feet and stood by a chair at 9 ½ months.

Began to walk about alone at 12 months . . .

While teething badly he would keep his hand in his mouth and bite on it.

. . . For months past a barrel organ has delighted him and he would start up on hearing one and go to the window at about 10 months, creeping there and lifting himself up to look through with his hands on the ledge.

New things have always delighted him, and he was even delighted when his father took him round to look at the pictures, gaselier etc and would smile at himself in glass.

. . . For months past he has amused himself with pointing out sheep and cows and birds on his nursery wall-paper, and now he utters a long "moo" when he sees a cow in the street.

. . . At 16 months he was much struck with a new tumbling man that was given him, standing and laughing at the top of his voice for minutes together. At first he seemed frightened of it as if he thought it were alive, but soon got over that.

He has recently learnt to sniff at flowers having been told to smell them. Without really smelling, he associates in his mind the sight of flowers and the action of sniffing and if taken in a room decorated with nosegays will stand and sniff all around for minutes together in a most amusing way.

. . . He has never been struck even lightly, and never punished, only spoken to. At about 12 or 13 months he tried to put one brick on another as he had seen done, but always preferred throwing down a castle, destruction being so much easier.

His legs are slightly bowed, as I fear he was allowed to walk too soon, but precautions are now being taken to get them right, eg whole wheat porridge, Trueman's sea salt, and high half boots.

He is very fond of using his limbs and always liked to be naked and have them free. At night now, when half stripped, he will run in endless circles round the nursery floor without getting giddy and stoop down and looking between his legs with his head on the floor . . .

February '84
23 months. Has for months been very fond of books, especially an illustrated Marjorie Fleming. Says "Daddy" now instead of "Dada" as formerly . . .

Very kind to his sister whom he calls "Mar" . . . Louise (his) nurse is "Ouce" shoes are "porries" handkerchief is "pompom" and he can now say scores of words more or less correctly . . .

Marjorie Mima Mander
Born March 2nd 1883

Biography begun July 3rd 1883

At 3½ weeks about 10 lbs

Had a good voice from first hour . . . being 8½ lbs in weight and having a large quantity of dark brown hair.

. . . Now at 4 months she looks about her a great deal . . . smiling when we smile and especially when her mother sings to her . . .

She watches Geoffrey running about with apparently great interest, and now begins to notice so much that she cries if left alone.

February '84

11 months. Gets up by herself to a chair and pushes it, and has done for some 2 or 3 weeks . . . Watches Geoffrey a great deal. Claps her hands when he does.

. . . Both she and her brother are very active and happy children.

28 Charlotte Street, Leamington. February 9th 1883

Dear Sir,

In answer to your inquiry the other day about our family history I'm sorry to say I can tell you very little. The William Mander to whom your letter was addressed was my Grandfather who died ten years ago. I believe he was born at Great Alne near Alcester in Warwickshire about the year 1786 and was registered at Aston Cantlow Church where some of the family are buried; his father was a farmer in that district, I think the name of the place was Alne Hill. One of the ancestors of this Great-grandfather of mine originally came from Holland with five brothers; one of these settled in Ireland and his descendants are the brewers who spell their name thus – Maunder; another brother settled near Alcester; the third brother cannot be accounted for but it is said that he went to reside at Brailes near Edge Hill. Although I am not quite sure about it, I may mention that my Grandfather had four or five brothers and several sisters whose descendants I have lost sight of. If you should find that we belong to the same family perhaps you would kindly let me know more about our connection as this is a matter in which I take great interest.

Hoping this small amount of information may be acceptable, I remain,

Yours faithfully, Yates Mander.

Brailes Vicarage, Shipston on Stour. 12 April '83

Dear Sir,

I am very much ashamed that your request for a search in our Parish Register has so long been neglected. Nothing but absolute inability to attend to it has caused this apparent discourtesy. I hope you will overlook it when you hear that ever since Christmas Day up to the beginning of March I was laid low by bronchitis. I have just returned from Ventnor in much better health but still very feeble.

A search through our old Register is no easy matter, as the ink is so much faded and the writing so bad that it requires a practised eye to find the required names. I have no one to whom I could look for help and have very carefully looked through the whole of the last century and not quite so particularly the century before and the only entries containing the name of Mander I can find are:-

- the Marriages of Wm. Maunder of Blockley and Jane Hobby of Brailes on November 22 1762,
- Wm. Maunder of Chipping Norton to Ann Turfley of Brailes on November 29 1796.

These are, I am pretty sure, the only entries in which the name of Mander occurs. If these are what you require I shall be happy to send certified copies of each. The fee is 3/7 but as I have really spent much time in the search, I trust you may feel disposed to help me a little in my wearisome and arduous task of restoring our grand old Church.

Believe me Dear Sir, Yours faithfully, T. Smith.

Brailes Vicarage, Shipston on Stour. 16 April '83
Dear Sir,

Accept my best thanks for your kind note enclosing cheque for one guinea.

As soon as I can spare the time I will go very carefully through our old Register and hope I may find the entries you desire. It will be very interesting if we can prove that your family tradition is well founded.

My daughters think they were at school with one or more of your near relatives at Miss Beyerhaus's, Wiesbaden. If correct, they desire to be very kindly remembered to their old school fellows.

Believe me Dear Sir, very faithfully yours, Thos. Smith.

A notebook from 1883 records a combined holiday and business trip spent in Scandinavia and Germany by Theodore and Flora. They left Wolverhampton on August 9th and travelling via Copenhagen and Goteborg, arrived in Christiania on August 20th

. . . Hotel Victoria (the best) full. Got good room at Hotel Scandinavie, very fair.

21st. Perambulated the town and found the streets and buildings very second rate, ditto the shops. Emil Larsen has a very good fur shop.

Situation of the town on the fiord, exquisite.

Visited the Dampkjokken[44] at midday and found thousands getting an excellent dinner at 25 or 40 ore apiece. Cooking is done by steam . . . Two stories very commodious. Long tables and benches . . .

Best thing in the town was Viking's Ship in a shed near the University. Found at Sandefiord. Dates from 9th. century . . .

24th. Stockholm Grand Hotel, very good.

After business and dinner, took coffee at the Strom-parterren[45]. Thence by little steam boat to Hasselbacken[45] and by carriage round the Djurgarden. Large park, poorly laid out. Shopped . . . Front room in hotel is important for the admirable view both by day and night over the water and town.

25th. Took steam boat at Riddarholmen at 9 am. Roamed over the straggling arms of the Malaren Lake, past Drottingholm etc to Upsala arriving at 3 pm.

. . . Interesting trip. Water way at times wide and rippling in the wind and sun, at others narrow as a canal.

At Upsala visited University; Cathedral containing tombs of Gustavus Vasa, and of Linnaeus . . .

26th. Attended English Church morning and evening . . .

27th. Noticed numerous Dalecarlian[46] peasants in their picturesque costume.

The following entry was written by Flora.

Visited the Institute of the Friends of Manual Labour, where are carried on various industries, weaving, embroidery, lace making etc.

Also the Northern Museum of Antiquities in Drottningatten . . . Annex 2 where most interesting relics of peasant life with interiors of houses are to be seen. Life like figures of peasants in costume.

To Riddarhaus where the Assembly of Swedish nobles meets. The walls are almost entirely covered with the coats of arms of the Swedish nobles . . .

Continued by Theodore

. . . National Museum, courteously explained to us (on an off-day) by an assistant of the curator Prof. Hildebrand . . . Very valuable and well ordered collection.

28th.
By Lake Malaren, by the Baltic and Gota canal to :-

29th. Motala
. . . Noisy boat while passing locks (37 to Motala!) Couldn't sleep.

30th.
3 am to 11 am Motala to Malmo. Kramer's Hotel, very good . . .

31st.
Steamer . . . Malmo to Stralsund . . . Latter town looks very quaint and pretty from the sea. Lofty churches and houses, old and picturesque. Train to Berlin. 11 am to 4.30 pm. Hotel de Rome . . .

September 4
After business travelled to Dresden. 5.15 – 8.15 express. Hotel Bellevue . . .

September 5
Visited Picture Gallery in the Zwinger. Best were – Murillo's and Raphael Madonnas . . . Angelica Kauffman's Vestal Virgin . . . Rembrandt's Head of an Old Man . . .

September 6
Visited the Grune Grewolbe, Kaufmann's Automatic musical instruments and the fine collection of Chinese, Japanese and Dresden porcelain in Johanneum.

. . . Beautiful music in the evening on the Bruhl Terrasse.

September 7
Steamer at 10. Noticed remarkable method of propelling tugs by chains, one for each direction, lying in bed of river and some 350 miles long, viz from Hamburg to Liebmaritz. Chain is drawn over cog wheels on steam tug's deck . . . Landed at Konigstein at 2 pm.

Dined and visited the most impregnable fortress. Train 5.30 to 10.20 to Prague . . .

September 8
Drove round this beautiful town . . . Rahthaus and ancient clock with 12 apostles, Death, skeleton and cock. Saw whole performance.

Market full of lovely flower wreaths . . . for Marie-fest. Churches full owing to saint's day.

The Jews' quarter, very ancient colony and graveyard.

University, the oldest in Germany . . . Radetsky monument . . . The Cathedral.

. . . The Burg or Imperial Palace with its historical Council Chamber and extremely beautiful Spanish hall, entirely white, chandeliers gold, seats red. Size 100 ft. long, 80 ft. wide, 40 ft. high . . .

Train 1.30 – 8.50 to Vienna. Imperial Hotel . . .

September 10
Dined at Zacher's behind the Hoftheater. Dear and very slow . . .

. . . Saw *exquisite* sculpture in white marble by Canova . . .

Drove in excellent two-horse shay . . . round Rings . . . saw many new and beautiful public buildings . . . These . . . which are fast making Vienna finest city in Europe, were built out of funds obtained by the sale of the site of the old fortifications, about 1872-6 . . . The sale realised some 40 millions of florin. This property was given to the city of Vienna on condition of its being built upon according to the directions of the Government . . .

Visited admirable Electric Exhibition where we heard an instrumental concert by telephone; also examined a suite of richly and tastefully decorated apartments charmingly lighted with different forms of electric lamp.

Drove back through a kind of semi-carnival, consisting of general illuminations, very many persons carrying Chinese lanterns, in celebration of the 200th. anniversary of deliverance of Vienna from Turks by John Sobiesky

September 12
Rail through Linz and Salzburg to Munich. 7.45 am – 6.30 pm.

September 14
Visited Bavarian National Museum. Very fine collection. Instruments of torture and old costumes most interesting. Complete and elaborate costume of a Huguenot lady who fled from France to Nuremberg.

Racks, thumbscrews, long-tongued masks for shrews, stocks, cat o' ninetails etc.

Drove to beautiful Southern cemetery . . . surrounded by elegant arcades.

Protestant and Catholic seemed to have compromised. Large cross at entrance and beautiful New Testament texts around its base. Catholics and Protestants buried there . . .

September 15
Train to Nuremberg 7 – 11 am.

. . . Drove all round the fortifications. Quaint old town but very dirty both to sight and smell.

Three squares lighted by carbon-point electric[47] lamp each and very effectively.

September 17
. . . Train to Frankfurt 2 pm – 8.30. Hotel – Frankfurter Hof, good but dear.

September 19
Flora in bed with cold.

September 20
. . . Wiesbaden. Visited Miss Beyerhaus . . .

September 21
Rail to Cologne and stayed the night there . . .

September 22
Rail to Rotterdam . . .

September 25
Rotterdam to Hague ½ hour express. Spent the day at the Hague and Scheveningen. Houses of Parliament, King's Palace. Picture Gallery . . . Long lines of fishing boats at Scheveningen. Beach chairs.

September 26
Drove round Rotterdam shopping . . .

September 27
. . . Rough passage.

London at 8 am Wood's Hotel. 3 to 4 hours at Gracechurch St. with H.C. Home at 7 pm.

Notes from a lecture on "The House Beautiful" given by Oscar Wilde[48] in Wolverhampton on March 10th 1884.

Rules in Art

1 Do not use anything which you do not know to be useful or think to be beautiful.
2 Do not use anything which you do not know to be a pleasure to yourself and which you do not believe was a pleasure to the workman who made it.

Colouring

. . . Fashionable colours are an error. It is as if one should say that B flat is to be the fashionable key of the season in music. All colours are beautiful but, as with tones, beautiful effect depends on their wise combination.

1884 diary of a holiday spent in Normandy by Theodore and his cousin Mander Smyth and a friend from Birmingham, Arthur Bayfield.

April 9
Took Flora, Geoff and Marjorie to Charing Cross for Tunbridge Wells to join Mother and Nellie and Lottie.

Myself, left Waterloo for Weymouth 2.15 – 6.12 pm where I joined M.J.S. and Bayfield. Left by 11.30 steamer for Cherbourg where we arrived at 6 am after an admirable passage.

April 10
Breakfasted at Hotel de France and after a very slight glance at the town with its imposing fortress and lively docks and quays, took train for Bayeux where we arrived in about 3 hours.

Extremely beautiful rural scenery all the way. Very English, being cut up into fields with hedges and trees . . . Gardens are numerous and extremely well cultivated, fruit trees occupying every good wall and every sunny hillside.

Bayeux, a charming old world town with quaint picturesque old houses, steep roofed and many windowed . . . The most notable thing in town is (the) famous tapestry 240 yards long by about 2½ feet wide, said to have been worked by Matilda, wife of W. Conqueror and her court ladies. It records visit of Harold to William in Normandy and subsequent conquest of England. It is kept in (a) museum and has considerable artistic merits.

Bayeux to Coutances. 3 hours by rail.

Still same picturesque and prosperous rural scenery. Every bank covered with primroses, with a frequent sprinkling of violets, hyacinths, wood sorrell and lady's smock and great golden masses of gorse and broom.

11th. Coutances. Hotel de France.
A quaint town most picturesquely situated on the top of a steep hill, approached by a long double avenue of limes. Attended service in grand old cathedral, made doubly beautiful by shining of sun through the stained glass windows of the chancel, lighting up double row of round pillars supporting lancet arches between chancel and lady-chapel.

The public garden, presented some 30 years ago by a private gentleman, is a charming resort for town's people. It is very sunnily situated and contains some exotics in open as well as glass. Camellias remain out all winter and a bank of sweet alyssum was in full flower like a bank of snow.

. . . Noticed in church ladies using charcoal footwarmers.

They travelled via Granville, to Dinan where they stayed over Easter weekend from April 12th to April 14th.

Hotel de Commerce. (Quaint, cosy and comfortable 7½ francs a day)
Town most charmingly situated . . . Surrounded by old walls, gates and fortresses and some fine avenues of trees . . .

Notabilia
Much less pronounced officialism than nearer Paris in orders and manners of railway guards, bus drivers etc . . .

Met a lady commercial traveller in hosiery trade and dined with her at table d'hote. It seems there are many lady commercials here.

Great picturesqueness in ordinary architecture of towns and especially in public buildings, even when they are quite plain.

An artistic neutral tone pervades buildings. Usual material is grey stone with tiles or small slates. Of course as population is nearly stationary there is very little building and so towns preserve their old-world appearance . . .

A bush of mistletoe instead of a sign where wine and cider are sold.

April 14
Today was fete de Lehon at Dinan, which is celebrated by natives and English

en masse, turning out and picnic-ing on banks of Rance.

We did not wait to see it owing to cold weather but drove by carriage about 15 kilometres from Dinan to Dinard . . .

Crossed bay by steamer to St Servan and stayed at Hotel de France et de Chateaubriand at St Malo (very good)

This quaint and old town being confined within ancient walls is cramped into narrow and very rambling streets. There is not one broad or straight one in town and consequently it is the easiest thing possible to get lost.

We walked almost round town on top of walls from which many varied glimpses of beautiful bay and neighbourhood are obtained.

15th. Train from St Malo to Pontorson . . . Walked . . . to Mount St Michel partly across sands 6 miles. Stayed chez Madame Poulard where we were very comfortable and fared excellently.

Mont St Michel 15th – 16th.
Vast expanse of sand. Sea out of sight at low tide. New (dyke) road of approach.

. . . Madame Poulard's excellent fare.

Chinese lanterns to light one up the rocky heights to bed.

Grand old church and monastery, 800 years old . . .

Met young English fellow coaching for army, viz. P.J. Miles of Odstock Rectory, Salisbury, also ex-barrister E.S. Cocks of Honiton.

Coach and train to Avranches . . .

Promenade under trees and platform giving wonderful view of surrounding country . . .

17th Train to Cherbourg. Hotel de l'Amiraute – good.
Very boisterous night so next (18th) morning took train to Paris. 8.30 – 5.30 Hotel Continental.

19th (From) Paris via Calais and Dover to Tunbridge Wells.

French local government items given by French fellow-traveller April '84

Every town has its "octroi" levied on foodstuffs and manufactured articles and devoted to municipal expenses. This is supplemented by direct taxation.

Whole country divided into Communes of which each, whether urban or *suburban* or *rural* has its "maire" elected by council and its council elected by ratepayers . . .

The next division in size to the Commune is the Canton, then the Arrondissement, and then the Department . . .

The Arrondissement is the basis of judicial administration . . .

In 1884 a notebook was begun in which the development of the garden at Mornington Place was recorded.

Gardener, Jones.

Warm dry summer, finest for 20 years.

German stocks bloomed freely. Single dahlias did tolerably well, rather too woody. Best rose year we have had here.

Borders very full and showy in August and September. Comparatively little blight, though others have suffered.

Gathered first cucumbers, grapes and tomatoes after middle of August, the rest mostly in September.

Total result:-

5 bunches of grapes, ripened very well.

Half dozen cucumbers, one 22 ins. long.

About half dozen marrows.

About half dozen custard marrows.

135 tomatoes, one weighed 6½ ozs.

two weighed 5 ozs each.

one weighed 10 ozs.

Seeds from Smith of Worcester.

Birmingham Daily Post, July 21, 1885.

Wolverhampton School of Art and School Board Offices.

. . . Yesterday the new School Board Offices . . . and the new School of Art in St. Peter's Close . . . were formally opened by the Right Hon. A.J. Mundella MP the (past) vice-president of the Committee of Council on Education.

. . . In the evening Mr Mundella . . . opened the new School of Art buildings. The ceremony was made the occasion of a conversazione given by the Mayor and Mayoress, the Art Gallery, which adjoins the new school, being thrown open for the purpose . . . Invitations . . . had been accepted by some 370 ladies and gentlemen . . . His Worship briefly opened the proceedings, and Mr S.T. Mander (the hon. sec. of the old school) then explained how the school came into existence. The old school in Darlington Street, he said, was opened in 1853 . . . Towards the new school the Education Department had promised the largest contribution that they were allowed to give – namely £1,000. (Applause.) Altogether £5,570 had been received by contributions and otherwise towards the building and stocking of the new school . . .

Mr Mundella M.P., who was well received, said there was no part of his official duties during the five years he was in office that he entered into with more zest . . . than the administration of the Science and Art Department. One reason, perhaps, for his zeal . . . was from a love of art, and from being one of those unfortunate beings whom people called collectors, who went about occasionally with cups and saucers in their pockets, and a plate under their arm, and who wasted their substance in old curiosity shops. (Laughter.) . . . He would relieve the mind of Mr Mander by telling him that he was sure the £1,000 required would be granted. (Hear, hear.) . . . Mr Joseph Jones moved a vote of thanks to the old School of Art Committee, coupled with the names of Major Loveridge and Mr Mander. He paid a high tribute to the energy and devotion to the new school, of Mr Mander. He was worthy of all honour – (applause) – for without his efforts the new school would never have been built. (Applause.)

Holiday diary

Antwerp and Switzerland July – August '85 Flora and self.

. . . (July) 26 Antwerp. Sunday.
Very hot. Excellent service at English church Rue de Tanneurs.

The city en fete for opening of new docks and quays, erected at cost of 4 million sterling. Saw King, also his daughter and her husband, Crown Prince of Austria.

Stayed at Hotel St Antoine. Very good.

Saw trades procession round the town – produce of all countries drawn by splendid teams of Flemish horses. English goods *not* well represented.

Music all day on Place Verte, sometimes by instrumental band, sometimes by singing societies of men. The latter, representing various towns of Belgium, very interesting, execution singular but excellent. I hear that they sing every Sunday.

July 27th Monday.
Spent 4-5 hours in Exhibition. Belgian, German, French, Austrian, Italian and Canadian sections very good. English very poor.

Most striking exhibits – Belgian lace dresses, lingerie, pottery and woodwork; French porcelain (Sevres etc.) Italian porcelain, mosaic, jewellery and glass.

The artistic character and fine taste of chief continental exhibits was quite remarkable.

July 28 Tuesday
Visited . . . the Picture Gallery with Flora . . .

Left about 4 and travelled via Brussels where we got a sleeping car divided up into very uncomfortably narrow sections, left it next morning at Bale and reached Lucerne about 11 am on –

July 29 Wednesday
Bale to Lucerne travelled with Captain Adam Smith of the Calcutta Volunteers, very pleasant man on his way out after short leave.

Schweizer-hof
Very large and good hotel. Officials not very obliging. Very hot . . . Met Rev. J.W. Rodger and 3 boys under his control.

Had 2 hours sail in boiling sun by steamer to Alpnach and back. Visited the town . . .

On Friday the 31st they travelled, via Brunnen, to Axenstein

Comfortable hotel, entertaining about 250 guests, very cosmopolitan, chiefly German.

German . . . 100, French . . . 30, Russian . . . 27, Italian . . . 26, English . . . 25, Dutch . . . 7, rest American, Austrian and Swedish etc.

Very beautiful fine woods surround the hotel, threaded by numerous paths. Air clear and bracing. View of Lake Pilatus etc. etc. unsurpassed on the lake. Place well worth staying at (for) some time, especially for invalids, though very few such were there.

Much of the next three days was spent taking long walks through the woods and sailing by steamer to places round the lake.

Tuesday August 4
Descended again to Brunnen. Steamer to Vitznau . . . to Kulm. Charming day and exquisite view. Saw two tame chamois and 4 St Bernard puppies belonging to a guide, Sebastian Spani. (Afterwards purchased one of the latter for 140 francs) During dinner a thunderstorm came on and the mountain was enshrouded in fog which prevented us from descending to Arth-Goldau.

On clearing, descended again to Vitznau in bright sunshine, wandered in that charming little village, with its luxuriant fig trees, geraniums and hydrangeas and returned by steamer to Brunnen and Aix.

People we met at Axenstein:-

Rev. Thompson S.P.G. chaplain.

Mrs Hollebone and three daughters from Kent.

Mr Ezechiel. Roman Catholic Jew from London – excellent pianist.

Entertained one evening by a boy of 8 who played most difficult pieces on the piano without music and with great ease and expression. Had learned only 3 years and practised 2-3 hours per day. Son of member of brass band.

Another evening 7 Italians played on string instruments with exquisite grace, skill and expression. No music. 3 violins, 2 cellos, 2 sort of guitars. Two of their number sang several Italian songs and whole joining in chorus and with string accompaniment. A perfect exhibition of native genius and taste . . .

Wednesday August 5

Took train to Brunnen and travelled thence . . . to Goschenen . . . carriage for 50 francs . . . through Andermatt, Hospenthal . . . to Rhone Glacier Hotel.

A very pleasant drive . . .

Thursday August 6

Visited end of Rhone Glacier now 1 mile from the hotel and fast receding. Grotto in solid blue ice, 140 feet long, very beautiful.

Carriage down Rhone Valley to Viesch (very hot) Sent heavy luggage on by post . . . Ascended, self on foot and Flora on horse and mule in 2½ hours to Eggishorn Hotel.

Friday August 7

Thunder and hail storm cleared the air and was followed by 3 marvellously bright and cloudless days . . .

Saturday August 8

Ascended Eggishorn . . . in 2 hours or less. Wonderful view including full 17 miles of great Aletschhorn glacier and a complete circle of snow covered peaks – Jungfrau, Eiger . . . Matterhorn etc. etc.

Flora spent 4 hours and lunched up there with a dozen or more others. A Mr Lloyd, a youth George Wright and I descended direct on to the Glacier, crossed its crumpled corner to further side . . . and returned over Marjelen Joch.

Interesting trip of altogether about 8 hours . . .

Met at Eggischorn Hotel:-

Rev. Glendinning of Christ Church, Woburn Square and chaplain to Marquis of Londonderry.

Mr Kyrle of Ledbury (invited us to call on him at home) Rev. Singer and wife, English chaplain at Lausanne and great climber.

Captain Bridge and sister, he just returned from 12 months campaign at Suakim.

2 Duffield brothers, one was stroke of Queen's boat while I was at Cambridge.

Signor Tomass de Cambray Diginy . . . and sister from Florence (another brother is just now mayor of Florence)

Rev. Wright (secretary of Church of England Temperence Society) wife, sister and daughter.

Mr and Mrs Douglas Fox, son and daughter. Engineer (Fox and Henderson)

Rev. Hardy, don of Sidney Sussex College, great climber, known as "King of Riffel."

Rev. and Mrs Faithful and 2 daughters from Edinburgh.

August 11

. . . Met Bishop Copplestone of Ceylon crossing glacier.

Wednesday August 12

An easy day. Wrote, read and talked.

Thursday August 13

. . . Visited two chalets built on slope. 2 rooms, kitchen behind on ground, sleeping rooms in part over cow shed and pig sty which give it some warmth . . .

We tasted some Neeb tea made from Iceland moss, wild camomile etc. Conversed with Prof. Tyndall[49] who lives at his house 5 minutes above the hotel for 2-3 months each year, up to the middle of October. Works land up there. Told me that the Aletsch Glacier moves . . . at rate of 19 in. per day opposite Eggisschorn and 8 in. near lower end . . .

He attributes goitre and cretinism to under feeding, unclean living, probably inter-marriage, but not to water.

Long walks were taken during the next few days: Flora stayed behind on Saturday when Theodore joined a party searching for Edelweiss in a walk that lasted for 8 hours.

Met at Bel Alp Hotel:-

Bishop Ellicott of Gloucester and Bristol, pleasant, talkative old man of 66.
Rev. and Mrs Hay Escott, rector of Kilve, Somerset. Very pleasant people.
Whittaker Escott, son of above, headmaster of Coventry Grammar School. Apparently about 37. (Another son is editor of Fortnightly Review.)
Professor Tyndall.
Mr Hoare[50], banker of London. Say, 50.
Mr and Mrs W Rathbone, M.P. for Caernarvonshire N. Agreeable people.
Rev. and Mrs Smethwick, vicar, Liverpool.
Mr Collett, son of Governor of Bank of England. Say, 27.
Mr and Mrs Norman, latter sister of Collett.
Mr and Mrs Cornish, clergyman.

The next day they began a journey by road, rail and steamer, arriving in Geneva on Wednesday August 19th.

. . . Hotel Metropole.

Called on Rev. and Madame Perluzon, Avenue de la Grenade. Monsieur very feeble, over 70, Madame very well and active.

Did much shopping!

Thursday August 20
Much more shopping.

St Bernard arrived from Rigi.

Visited cathedral, Botanical gardens etc. Also:-

Ecoles des Arts Industrieles
Large building recently erected by state (in 1878) and maintained by it in order to encourage flagging industries of town and country. All instruction free. For ladies an entrance exam required.

62 men (mostly young) 100 ladies, now under instruction.

Orders taken and executed. Show-rooms of works and one for sale.

4 or 5 professors.

Modelling in plaster and wax.

Modelling and decoration of porcelain (baked on the premises)

Stone carving.

Wood carving.

Metal chasing and repousse work, other branches to be added.

Manufacturers send here for their art workmen.

All elementary drawing is taught in about half a dozen free art schools built and supported by town of Geneva and holding classes from 6-10 am and from 6-8 pm.

There is also a municipal Ecole de l'Horologerie.

Left by 8 pm train for Paris and London.

1885 September 1

Geoffrey	Height	3 ft. 2½ ins	Weight	34 lbs. 7 ozs
Marjorie	"	3 ft. 1 in	"	29 lbs

Summer clothes and thin shoes.

Garden

Very fine exhibition of polyanthuses in April from last year's seedlings.

In the late winter planted 16 roses from Prince of Oxford in ground prepared on H.G. Tippet's instructions. Well drained with one foot of stones and brick ends.

July. Several of the above roses . . . are flowering freely . . . Very good rose year.

July 9
Noticed a fly-catcher and cat watching each other at my front gate. The bird, anxiously twittering, descended 4 times towards the cat, generally striking it with wings or beak, both when the bird was on the wall and on the ground.

August 1
Gathered first tomatoes (Seeds from Smith of Worcester)

August 8
7 tomatoes weight 1 lb. 9 oz

September 3
12 tomatoes weight 1 lb. 13 oz. one = 9 oz.

October 1
Total = 165 tomatoes weight = 37 lbs Average = 3.58 oz.

Grapes . . . 35 bunches in all but they withered from some unknown cause before maturity. Chrysanthemums . . . Blooming commenced in mid November and lasted through December.

Heat was gently applied in December.

Visitors' book[51] *– Mornington Place 1885*

Name – Henry N. Paint Address – Ottawa. Canada. August 2nd to October 22nd.

Notes on emigration to Canada followed the 1885 entry in the garden notebook. The information probably came from Flora's father and sister Mary; the initials "H.N.P." and "M.P. September 3/85" head the first page.

Cost of passage from Liverpool to Winnipeg = $25 per adult, children less.

Agents put emigrants through and help them in finding work near their allotments of 100 acres. Children put out, over say 10 years, to farmers' families.

Emigrants fed on way out and are found in seed and a few tools, (not oxen or ploughs. This is done but not guaranteed.) Farmers share ploughs and work at first.

Agent in Liverpool – Mr Baker

Agent in Quebec – Mr Stafford (write [to] him. H.P. knows him)

James Beatty M.P. for Toronto . . . has 600 miles of line to build N.W. from Winnipeg . . . He wants both navvies and settlers. H.P. could speak to him.

Alex McNeill M.P. for Bruce, philanthropic man, might find work for 20.

H.P. might speak to J.H. Pope M.P., Minister of Agriculture . . . and get a grant in aid of say $5 per head, possibly.

Emigrants have a hard time at first, but hardly any at all succumb. Can plant all they want and keep them at once eg wheat, potatoes, parsnips, turnips, carrots.

Can get 2 bushels of wheat for a day's work from a farmer.

Flour to be had everywhere from storekeepers, in exchange for wheat.

Tents to be bought everywhere.

Emigrants sometimes excavate holes and cover them and live in at first. The farmers who want their labours will supply tents etc.

Time to go:- April.

Garden 1886

August . . . Coreopsis is doing very well . . . also seedling carnations of different kinds. Roses flowered pretty freely.

Cucumber 1 lb 3 oz.

Architect's drawing of Wightwick Manor 1887, showing on the right the single storey billiard room which was demolished when the 1893 extension was added.

In 1887 Theodore and Flora bought Wightwick Old Manor from the Hinckes family and commissioned the Liverpool architectural firm Grayson and Ould to design a new house to be built in the grounds.

Report on a visit to Spearpoint [52]*, a house in Ashford. Kent. April 1887.*

Built on foundations of old farmhouse and partly incorporated.

Lower part rough-cast, upper part weather tiled.

General appearance very neat and comfortable.

All windows long and low with smallish panes; too small.

Window sashes and doors painted deal and shrunk.

Drawing room 9 ft. 6 high.

Dining room 9 ft. high. Not too low.

Hall very pretty. Wide staircase with pretty turned balusters.

Hall open to second storey.

Walls inlaid with crossed old oak beams, very effective.

Stair carpet, plain sapphire blue Brussels with flat brass stair rods, very pretty.

Did not care for design of mantel shelves. Cross bar of windows too low in dining (and) in drawing rooms.

Mantel shelves and tiling, ref. fireplaces, not so pretty as Ould's.

Stables en suite and very pretty.

No half timber except in gables and that plain oak.

Garden at Mornington Place 1887
June 4 Lilies only just out, Laburnums in full bud.

First contract instalments paid towards building the new house.

Henry Lovatt, Darlington Street, Wolverhampton. Received from Grayson and Ould, 31 St James' Street, Liverpool for work and materials used in contract:-

29 October 1887 . . . £600
7 December 1887 . . . £500

Grayson and Ould, Architects.
Received on account of architect's commission:-

31 October 1887 . . . £30
22 December 1887 . . . £100

Henry Lovatt received further payments of £1,550 between January and the end of May 1888.

Garden 1888

April (early) 5 cwt. ground bones and 2 cwt salt per acre on grass land at Wightwick.

May 10 First game of tennis (Mornington Place.)

May 12 13 nests in 4 trees in rookery at Wightwick. Young rooks just getting on the wing. Shot 11 (Adams, Howard and self)

Lionel Henry Mander was born on May 14th.

May 14 Lionel weighs 11 lbs.

June 14 Flora weighs 141 lbs.
July 5 Flora weighs 152 lbs after 3 weeks in Malvern.
Lionel 7 weeks old. Flora's previous usual weight 120 lbs.

Garden

July 9 First plate of strawberries gathered at Wightwick.

July 11 First peas from Wightwick

From June to November 1888 Henry Lovatt was paid £750 every month: the instalment for August was divided between "house £400" and "farm £350"

Items purchased by Edward Ould towards furnishing Wightwick Manor

December 20th 1888.

Etching "The Harvest Moon"	£3 0.0
Etching for Boudoir	£0. 16.0
Old Grate	£0. 12.0
Packing and cartage of same	£0. 5.0
Two Tyne castle (sic) Tapestry figures in Bedroom chimney piece and decoration of same	£0. 9.0
	£5. 2.0

Commission paid to Edward Ould on December 20th – £200

Garden 1889

Wightwick
March Put vegetable mould from cleansing of both pools done last autumn and mixed with gas lime on Jackamore and Arycroft . . .
May 4 First swallow.

May 1 – 7 Took up north half of tennis lawn because soft and wet, and relaid it on 2 in. black ashes and 1 in. red sand on top.

June 2 At 7 am the severest hail-storm known for many years, with thunder and lightning, visited the neighbourhood. Our roses, herbaceous plants, seedlings, peas etc. etc. suffered seriously, the garden being put back 3 weeks.

In many places crops were badly damaged, especially fruit, and much glass broken.

It has been a stormy season and a week ago I noticed meteoric stones scattered about the pavements in town about as large as cherry stones.

In 1889 Henry Lovatt received two payments of £750, one in January and the other in April. The last recorded payment was £500 made to him in July. Excluding £350 paid towards the farm, the total expenditure on the house at this time appears to have been £8,630. [53]

Notebook containing reports on visits to 15 art schools in Europe.

Ecole Municipale du Dessin, Molenbeck St. Jean, Brussels.
Suburb forming a separate Commune or municipality of 40,000 inhabitants, all poor.

Fine building erected by the Commune at the cost of and maintained by the same . . .

Concierge and wife receive 900 francs per year.

Chief director 3,000 francs, others in proportion.

500 pupils and 200 more on the list cannot get in.

Instruction free to inhabitants of the Commune, but they find their own materials.

Students (apparently all boys) from 8 years upwards. Attend primary school during day and Art school at night.

On entering, draw with chalk on blackboard, then with charcoal on paper.

Mostly stand to their work. Apparently do not draw from flat, but outline from the cast and then from groups of models or natural objects.

Hang board on the wall and work on it vertically or pull out bottom end . . . on their knees sitting down on a stool.

Each student has his own gas jet with shade, also another jet with shade to light the object . . .

Almost all students of the artisan class . . .

There are several communal schools in suburbs of Brussels but Molenbeck said to be best.

A prize of 600 francs is given at Molenbeck school each year to the best student and with this he travels in England, France or Germany and at length presents a report of his work . . .

Academie des Beaux Arts, Rue Boulevard du Midi.
In an old monastery.

Very large and well provided school. 800 students and some 200 more seeking admission, mostly from city but a few from a distance . . .

Students begin young but owing to large number applying they have to pass an entrance exam.

Tuition was free until this year but now a uniform charge of 5 francs per month is made either for day or evening instruction, as they think the instruction is more valued when paid for . . .

Students were artists and workmen of various trades but apparently all young, ie. under about 21, except in the advanced classes . . .

In another large room were a number modelling from the life, two figures, a man and a boy in one case, standing in a group, and on the other side of the room, a man alone.

They pay the models 5 francs for an evening of 2 hours.

. . . The work lasts from 7 to 9 and then there is often a lecture afterwards until 10, and these fellows are mostly at work all day!

Ecoles des Arts Industrielles et Decoratifs.
. . . Noticed that special instruction was given in graining to imitate various marbles (large slabs of marble being provided) also in carriage construction, drawing and in carving wood, stone and marble.

Kunst Museum, Dusseldorf.
Large and pretentious building. Here as elsewhere there is far too much imitation, eg the columns and walls of the entrance hall appeared to be of splendid red and green marble, which turned out to be grained and varnished wood.

Kunst-Gewerbe Schule and Museum, Koniggratzer Strasse, Berlin.
A magnificent, most elegant building, founded by Crown Princess and now carried on by government. A copy of South Kensington but a finer building although not so extensive.

. . . School attached. 500 students all but 20% of whom pay . . .

House painters study here.

90 Koniggratzer Strasse.
A society maintained by private subscriptions for the training of several hundred young girls in several branches of instruction by which they may maintain themselves.

Rooms rather cramped so the girls have to be divided into several successive classes in the same subject.

Saw classes being taught sewing, cutting out, embroidery, artificial flower making, drawing, painting and design.

Work done is sold and orders taken.

Ecole des Beaux Arts, Paris.
Very extensive and splendid school for artists, sculptors and architects . . .

Each year a "Prix de Rome" is awarded to the best students.

Its value is £500 to £600 and he is required to travel to Italy and live 4 years or so doing good work.

Each year's first prize is kept in painting and modelling and there is now a large collection of these.

Anyone can come and draw from the various casts etc. in the large courts and galleries and we noticed many doing so, including several who were serving their time as soldiers.

Garden 1890

February Willcock rebuilt wall in lane opposite Uncle H. [54] Enlarged lower pool by about six yards in widest part.

March Slack left. Bishop came (gardener)

Planted ground near pools with pines, fir, spruce etc. etc . . .

July/August No damsons, very few apples and pears. Strawberries all July abundant and good from potted runners and all netted 3 ft. high.

Not a good rose season, so much blight and green fly. Asters and many other plants suffered similarly. Stocks, sweet williams, nasturtiums, summer chrysanthemums and poppies very good.

In 1891, after serving on the council for 10 years, Theodore became an Alderman.

Alan Jocelyn Mander was born on January 28th.

January 28 Alan weighs 9¼ lbs

March 7 Flora 142 lbs, Alan six weeks old

Garden 1891

April Fruit house finished (Richardson of Darlington) [55]

May 17 Whit-Sunday A heavy fall of snow. Trees in full leaf covered densely – a beautiful sight, ground covered 2 in. deep.

1892

February 2
Took Mrs Wright's land from Uncle Harper for a year at £50.

March 25
Took Col. Loveridge's farm buildings at nominal rental of £1 . . .

April 5
Dismantling part of orchard for building and making terrace on west of house with the soil . . .

Cheque book stub – January 5 1893

H. Willcock to Repairs Mornington Place . . . £22. 5s. 3d.

Paragraph from Building News 1893

Addition to Wightwick Manor.
It is only about four years since Messrs. Grayson and Ould built this house in the old timber style for Mr S.T. Mander in the country near Wolverhampton, but they have now been employed to build an addition to it, which is as large as the entire house originally built. This consists of a hall or "great parlour" about 50 ft. by 21 ft. with an open panelled roof and minstrels' gallery, a billiard-room, dining room, secondary staircase and servants' offices, with bedrooms over all but the parlour. The style adopted is again the black and white, but it is more massive as well as more ornate than the original structure. The chimneys are twisted, of South Country brick, from Mr James Brown of London. Messrs. Rattee and Kett, of Cambridge supplied the oak work, and the contractor is Mr Henry Willcock of Wolverhampton.

Garden 1894

Very mild winter. Hunting not stopped more than a fortnight all through season.

February Severest storm known for years. Lost 8 trees, including elm before the house. Unusually windy weather Jan/March . . .

April 26 . . . Put new wire fence down rookery walk from opposite drawing room window to gate by upper pool.

Cutting from local paper

Bazaar at Wightwick Manor.
The charmingly arranged grounds at Wightwick Manor, the residence of Mr S.T. Mander, were wisely chosen for a bazaar in aid of the Orphan Home, . . . the opportunity of viewing the . . . gardens being an attraction no ordinary bazaar could boast of. The bazaar was gracefully opened today by the Countess of Dartmouth. [56] Mrs S.T. Mander was the originator of the affair, and at much personal trouble and inconvenience she arranged the whole of the

proceedings. The bazaar was held in one of the large reception rooms at Wightwick Manor, and no prettier contrast could have been devised than the old oak adornments of the walls and the delicate tinted fabrics that decorated the stalls . . .

In the 1890's a small school was established by Theodore in the Malt House adjoining the old Wightwick Manor and his children, their cousins and friends were pupils there: a school magazine was started, edited by the teacher, [57] *and all the numbers for 1894-1895 were bound into one volume.*

Editorial from the school journal February 1895

Topical Notes
. . . Nearly all our members have lately been having a very trying, and yet at the same time, most delightful week of Ice. Skates have been begged, borrowed or stolen and the temporary or proper owners have been skimming gaily along the frozen canal.

Well do we remember the ear piercing cries which were uttered when a poor unfortunate fell.

How we laughed when several performers kissed Mother Ice in a miscellaneous heap of arms and legs . . .

Some of our members too have been coasting, sleighing and tobogganing, but not down the front staircase this time but over the firm, white, glistening snow.

Garden 1895

Severest winter for 50 years.

Hunting stopped for whole of January and February Frost and snow all the time.

Temp of 2° or 3° below zero recorded at Wightwick, and of 23° below zero = 55° of frost in Scotland.

Many water mains frozen 2 and 3 feet below ground.

Shrubs terribly injured.

March 24 Terribly severe storm of short duration. Worse than that of last spring. Lost 16 trees, while scores came down in the neighbourhood: Patshull lost 1,000, Apley[58] 500, Davenport[58] its avenue . . .

Wightwick Manor photographed in 1895.

Wightwick school photograph. Marjorie is standing on the far left with Alan (curly hair) seated in front of her. Lionel is sitting on the rug on the right.

Wightwick School Journal May 1895

Topical Notes
Measles – Greatly has been the anxiety and fear lately since this prostrating and malignant disease has made its appearance . . . Peeps have been taken at the invalids, and other members may be glad to know that they looked remarkably well.

Midland Liberal Federation, Central Offices, Atheneum Chambers,
71 Temple Row, Birmingham. June 26 1895
Dear Sir,

The Liberals of Mid-Worcester are very anxious to secure a candidate and they believe with some reason that there is an excellent prospect of success if the right man be found.

I have ventured to suggest that they should seek an interview with you on the subject.

Your name would be known and you have almost a local connection. The organization has been fairly well maintained and the registration attended to. The constituency is really Liberal in tendency and is not difficult to work.

I trust you will not refuse to listen to the suggestion.

I am yours faithfully, William Woodings.

Garden Notebook

Shooting

1895 September
Took out first game licence.

September 21
Shot partridges for first time. Trysull with B.H.M.[59] Fine hot day . . . Killed 1½ brace.

September 27
Held a croquet tournament in broiling hot weather.

Day temperature 75° in the shade.

Evening 7.30 quite dark, 69° in front of the house.

This weather has now lasted 6 weeks and is unprecedented in September.

Ground very hard and dry. No scent. Cub-hunting suspended for the first time on record in the Albrighton Hunt.

Flora and Theodore, Lionel and Alan in the Wightwick sleigh.

1896
Left home for 10 weeks on trip with Flora to Ceylon. On return could not shoot owing to dysentery taken in Ceylon.

1896 December 25th

Geoffrey	4 ft 10
Marjorie	5 ft 3
Lionel	4 ft 4
Alan	3 ft 11

Garden 1897

March . . . Razed cottages beyond canal . . . Finished three new cottages on Bridgnorth Road and altered 4 old ones on Wightwick hill early last autumn and planted fruit trees in the gardens and mountain ashes by Dunn's in this spring . . .

Extracts from a notebook kept by Geoffrey from 1896 – 1899.

Wightwick village

Mr Joseph Dunn m. Miss Boudler

Children: Mary, Joseph, Ellen, George.

Wightwick Manor Servants.

House keeper (1898)	Henrietta Broome
Housemaids..................................	Alice Mann, Annie Maddocks
Cooks etc......................................	Miss Cardwell
Butlers...	James Chopping

Footmen	George Pugh, James Smallwood
Nurses	Helen Prince
Stables/coachmen	Joseph Morris
Cowmen	J. Walton (d. September 18 1898) J.Gardner
Engineer	J. Dunn
Gardens etc	
Head gardeners	George Bishop (left 1897) Frank King
Under Gardeners	James Hemmings, William Winter, Richard Palmer
Grooms	E.Tudge, Gidian Hule

Garden 1899

January 24
Very mild winter til today. Unusually wet and stormy month. Hard frost and fine weather began today.

Young thrush, apparently fortnight old, seen on lawn today!

April 18
Lionel found thrush and blackbird eggs in same nest. They were also seen by me (S.T.M.)! Don't know how they got there . . .

Eight herbaceous beds before drawing-room window planted this spring, taking place of a shrubbery.

April 22
Restocked two small pools in Netherton[60] garden a month ago, with 200 yearling trout and 1,000 fry, brown and rainbow. 50 large ones taken out and put into old fish pond.

7 First Avenue, Brighton. 29th. July 99
Dear Mr Mander,

As promised I now enclose you a formal letter in reference to our fee in connection with the proposed alterations and additions to the gardens at Wightwick Manor. I calculate that it would take 2 years to finish our work in the garden, that that the work would entail *most* careful thought and planning and that a great deal of personal supervision would be necessary. I estimate that the travelling and out of pocket expenses which we should incur during the progress of the work would amount to *at least 50 Guineas.* In the event of your accepting our terms, I suggest that Mr Parsons[61] and I go down very shortly to Wightwick – thoroughly discuss all matters connected with the garden and then submit you a rough plan of what we advise should be carried out, with any remarks necessary thereon – a patched up job is never satisfactory, and is always the most costly in the long run, and I would strongly advise you, if you alter the gardens in any way, to make a thorough job of it so that the results will prove a permanent success once a good and feasible scheme is settled on, the work can be done bit by bit so that the grounds may be tidy and in order next summer, this I gather is your wish.

The alterations we should advise being carried out would involve little expense in the way of constructive work, and would tend to decrease the labour in the garden. Our object is to make the grounds much more compact and less rambling and disjointed than at present.

I have included Mr Parsons' preliminary fee and his and my . . . travelling expenses already incurred, in the fee quoted in our formal letter.

Yours truly, W. Partridge.

7 First Avenue, Brighton. 29th. July 99
Dear Sir,

The Gardens, Wightwick Manor

We undertake to prepare and submit the plans and designs necessary to carry out the alterations and additions to the above, to superintend the carrying out of these works, and to direct and advise on all matters connected thereon for the sum of Two Hundred and Fifty Guineas (£262.10.0) This fee to include all our travelling and out of pocket expenses.

We are Dear Sir, Yours faithfully, Parsons and Partridge

Visitors' Book

Name –	W. Partridge	Address – Caversham	August 25/26 '99
	Alfred Parsons	London	

Wolverhampton Express and Star.

Mr Theodore Mander's Public-House
What he Intends to do With it.
Mr Theodore Mander, B.A., J.P., . . . has purchased the Mermaid Inn[62], Wightwick, which is near his residence, Wightwick Manor, and this afternoon . . . he applied to the magistrates . . . to sanction plans for extensive alterations to it. The inn is to be enlarged and conducted on the method of the People's Refreshment House Association Limited . . . and . . . is to be conducted as a house of refreshment instead of a mere drinking bar. Food and non-intoxicating drink shall be exposed for sale on the counter. Drink, both intoxicating and non-intoxicating of the best quality is to be sold, and the manager will have the profit on the non-intoxicating drink only. Part of the inn will be used as a public

house, and the other part will be reserved for cyclists and persons who will partake of tea. Adjoining the inn Mr Mander will erect a village reading-room where no intoxicating drink will be supplied. The Magistrates granted the application . . .

The Mayor of Wolverhampton 1899

Wolverhampton Express and Star Tuesday November 9th 1899

Mayor's Day Wolverhampton
The space reserved for the public in our Council Chamber today was fully occupied with an attendance of leading residents of the borough, the fair sex,

as usual, largely predominating, to witness the ceremony of electing a member of the Council to fill the office of Mayor of the borough for the ensuing year, in succession to the retiring mayor, Alderman Price Lewis . . .

Punctually at twelve o'clock the retiring Mayor wearing the robes and official gold chain, entered the Council Chamber and at once announced that the first business was the Election of a Mayor . . .

Alderman W.H. Jones, in rising, was greeted with applause. He said "it gives me great pleasure to nominate a gentleman as Mayor who, I believe, will receive the unanimous vote of the Council. I mean Mr Alderman S. Theodore Mander J.P." (applause) . . .

Chapel Ash, Wolverhampton November 10 1899
My dear Nephew,

Allow me to congratulate you on your appointment as Chief Magistrate. I have no doubt you will be able to justify the expectations entertained of your ability faithfully, to discharge all its duties and to shed additional lustre in the old town.

It was my intention to join the procession of Volunteers and accompany you to church, sad recent events rendered it more prudent for me now not to think of this.

My nephew Lyle called upon me today and informed me that Paul wrote to him in August last that he did not consider his wife of sound mind; there must have been, in my opinion, some great provocation.

Yours affectionately, John Fraser.

23 Henrietta Street, Cavendish Square, London. W. November 10 1899
My dear Theodore,

You have been much in my mind the last few days and I write to congratulate you upon your honours and to express the hope that all needed strength and wisdom may be given you for your very arduous duties . . . I wish that my father could have lived, as he often told me that he so looked forward to your term of office and the expectations he had of your success.

You would, I know, have had his prayers – you have mine as well as Mary's . . .

I am affectionately yours, Robert W. Felkin.

The Midland Evening News December 1899

Accident to the Mayor of Wolverhampton
Thrown from His Trap
An accident that was happily unattended with serious results happened to the Mayor of Wolverhampton (Alderman S. Theodore Mander) on Tuesday

evening. His Worship was driving down Darlington Street at about half past nine, and was following the tramcar which left Queen Square . . . for Tettenhall. He was alone in the trap. When opposite the Tramway Company's stables a person stepped off the car in front of the Mayor's trap, and in the sudden effort to pull up and avoid running over the thoughtless individual who thus exposed himself to unnecessary risk, Alderman Mander's horse lost its footing and fell. His Worship was thrown out and alighted in the road, but most fortunately he was not injured beyond a shaking, and quickly took his seat in the trap again and drove on. The foolish person who was the cause of the mishap had a very narrow escape, and was only saved from a serious accident by the Mayor's vigorous promptitude in stopping his horse.

The family at Wightwick in the mid 1890's

Newspaper cuttings

January 9th. 1900
An appeal to Canadians
Sir, – I have received a notice from the office of the High Commissioner of Canada intimating that a small committee has been formed in London, for the purpose of raising funds to provide additional comforts for the Canadian contingents in South Africa. It is not proposed to invite donations from the general public, but only from Canadians living in the United Kingdom, and from

those who are intimately and directly connected with the Dominion. Colonel Otter, commanding the first Canadian contingent already in South Africa, was informed of the action in contemplation and requested to state what it might be most desirable to send. His reply was:- "Many thanks from Canadians. Compressed meat and lime-juice most acceptable."

It is also suggested that woollen socks, helmets, Tam o'Shanters and underclothing should be sent.

. . . Anyone willing to knit socks or helmets may receive, on application to me, simple and accurate directions for making the same. May I ask that a ½d stamped and addressed envelope be enclosed with each application.

Faithfully yours, Flora St Clair Mander. Mayoress of Wolverhampton.

April 28th. 1900

The Queen in Wolverhampton[63].
Her Majesty the Queen has during the midnight hours passed through Wolverhampton on many occasions on her journeys to and from Balmoral . . . but . . . when it was known that the train on which she was being conveyed from Holyhead to London would reach Wolverhampton about half past two yesterday afternoon the greatest excitement prevailed and . . . the bridges and other points of advantage along the line . . . were crowded with people . . .

. . . The Mayor and Mayoress accompanied by their three children, Miss Marjorie, Master Lionel and Master Alan, the last named in full Highland dress . . . were upon the platform of the Low Level Station shortly after two o'clock . . . The platform was covered with red cloth and decorated with plants provided by the Mayor. Punctually to time the Royal train steamed in and during the seven or eight minutes halt required for changing engines, her Majesty, having previously intimated that she would receive a bouquet from the Mayoress, invited her into the carriage, and the Mayoress, having presented a basket of roses, her Majesty graciously accepted them, and said, "I thank you. You are very kind," and shook hands with the Mayoress . . .

The Mayor and Town Clerk were next introduced, after which the train moved out amidst loud cheers . . .

Crowds of people congregated at various points in Birmingham commanding a view of the line along which the Royal train travelled

. . . The train passed through without slackening speed, and it was impossible to distinguish any of the occupants except the Indian attendants . . .

At half-past five the Royal train reached Windsor. At Windsor where they know the Queen better than she is known anywhere else in England, the citizens awaited her appearance with curiosity, to see whether she really looked as well as everybody has been saying. They confirmed the general verdict.

30 Loanhead Terrace, Aberdeen 28th. April 1900.
Madam,

I am very much obliged to you for your kind letter and in answer beg to say that I have only just left Mrs Charrington, Somerford Manor, Wilts. with whom I lived 5½ years as Lady Housekeeper and received as salary £50 . . . I assisted Mrs Charrington with her business correspondence, arranged her flowers, and did all her principal needlework for the house including the mending of her best bed and table linen.

My age is 45 years and I am Scotch.

It will perhaps be best for both that I should at first go to you, as you suggest, temporarily.

The Dowager Lady Lockheart Ross of Malnagowrie with whom I lived 18½ years has asked me to go next Tuesday to help her to engage servants and to arrange her London house for the season, and to stay on with her till suited with a situation, but I am sure should you want me before being able to accomplish what she asks me to do, she would wish me to go to you.

I remain Madam, Yours faithfully, Emma Smith.[64]

P.S. After Tuesday my address will be:-

c/o Lady Lockheart Ross, 18 Wellington Court, Albert Gate. S.W.

Melbury, Dorchester May 2nd.
Madam,

I have only received your letter this morning forwarded on to me from home. I am delighted to answer any question you may care to ask regarding Miss Smith. She is most perfectly honest and reliable in every respect. During the years she was with me I trusted her with everything from my personal valuables down to the complete household effects. She is the most methodical worker and manager and ever willing to put her hand to anything – she is also a good accountant and excellent needlewoman. While in my service she acted both as housekeeper and secretary, writing all my letters and business etc. She arranges flowers beautifully and understands keeping a house in perfect order. She gets on well with the servants and is a pleasant retiring person, who never puts herself forward and considers everyones wishes before her own. I may safely say that she is honest and reliable in every single respect, and as a proof of this, I may add that she wrote all my cheques, paid everything and everyone and was trusted to the very fullest extent by everyone who knew her. Any other questions you may think of and may care to ask I shall be happy to reply to, as I cannot say too much for Miss Smith's excellent qualifications.

Believe me, Yours faithfully, Monica L. Charrington.

The visit of the Chinese Ambassador and his party to Wolverhampton. The group was photographed outside the front door at Wightwick.

Newspaper cuttings

Tuesday May 8, 1900.
Wolverhampton has entertained a distinguished visitor yesterday and today, in the person of Sir Chih Chen Lofengluh, the Chinese Ambassador. It is only recently that we have heard of China and the "open door," . . . the Ambassador himself proclaimed the policy within our own Town Council Chamber yesterday. "You know" said his Excellency, "that China is now quite open to you for your trade, and that you have always the open door of hospitality and instruction." That is an announcement which elicited . . . a ringing cheer.

In the course of the visit one of the members of the Council ventured a remark . . . that from what he had read . . . the custom, once so prevalent in China, of binding up the feet of the female sex . . . was gradually being given up in . . . principal parts of the Chinese Empire.

"Ah!" replied the attaché "I have no doubt you English people consider that a very cruel practice. You allow your ladies in this country more freedom of action in that respect?"

"Most certainly" said the gentleman . . .

"But" added the attaché (with a merry twinkle in his eyes) "I have noticed during my residence in this country that your . . . fashionable ladies have very small waists . . . And I was interested to learn how they accomplished it. And I was informed that the contraction of their waists was brought about by compressing them within a kind of steel cage – I think you call them corsets . . . Your ladies with their small waists certainly look very pretty . . . To my idea however, it seems rather a cruel practice to prevent Nature developing herself . . . in that way. You doubtless greatly admire your ladies small waists, and so . . . we also admire our ladies' small feet." I think my readers will agree that the attaché turned the tables very neatly on his too inquisitive inquirer.

May 1900

The Royal Visit to Wolverhampton
. . . their Royal Highnesses the Duke and Duchess of York have graciously consented to visit Wolverhampton in the month of July next, to distribute the prizes to the successful scholars at the Wolverhampton Orphanage, and to open the new Infirmary now in the course of erection . . .

As soon as it became known that Wolverhampton was to be honoured with a Royal visit, a desire was expressed by the civic authorities that their Royal Highnesses should also . . . be prevailed upon . . . to lay the foundation stone of the new Municipal Free Library, which is to stand as the town's permanent memorial of the Queen's Diamond Jubilee . . .

We are now officially informed by the Mayor that . . . the Duke and Duchess of York will be pleased to comply with the request made.

Hotel Kaiserhof, Schutzenstr. 12 Munich.
21/5/1900
Friday evening 10 pm.
Dear Mother,

We have arrived here safely and so far are all right. We left Frankfurt at 11.08 pm and arrived Munich 7 am. We had no sleeping car, but I managed to sleep a good deal in my seat . . . It has been raining here all day, but still we have managed to get through 4 Art Galleries, and have 1 more tomorrow. Munich is a very poor town compared with Frankfurt; in fact I think Frankfurt must be one of the most delightful towns in Germany, clean, fine buildings, delightful surroundings, one of the most perfect sanitary systems in the world and excellent water from the mountains and last, but not least, an inimitable tram service . . .

We leave here tomorrow, Saturday . . . for Oberammergau reaching there about 7 pm . . . leave after Passion Play Sunday evening and reach Munich 11 pm. Leave via Verona for Venice . . . Monday if all goes well . . .

I am sorry to say that my camera never really recovered from the shock received in getting lost in Cologne and is now quite done up and I cannot use it . . . I will try and get the autographs for Marj. but I have not much time to spare . . . I am wearing my German squash hat in my travelling so do not be surprised if you see a suspicious looking German wandering about Wolverhampton . . . You will probably receive a notice from Cooks about our luggage as we have despatched it to Wolverhampton, Wightwick Manor and have only our small handbags with us . . .

From your loving son, Geoffrey L. Mander.

Richmond House, 49 Portland Place (London) W. June 13 1900
Dear Mrs Mander,

I thank you very much for your letter of the 7th. inst., and should feel obliged if you would be so good as to present to Miss Gordon Cumming my acknowledgements for her kindness in sending me a copy of her book explanatory of her system of teaching illiterate and blind Chinese to read their language in a much shorter time than by the method now in vogue.

The system is most ingenious, and must be a great boon to those whose education has, for some reason or another, been neglected in their youth.

Please remember me kindly to your husband and believe that I preserve a very pleasant souvenir of all the kind attentions shewn me by you and him on the occasion of my recent visit to Wolverhampton.

Yours very truly, Sir Chih Chen Lofengluh (Chinese Ambassador)

Newspaper cuttings

Tuesday July 3 1900
The Royal Visit
The Street Decorations
A meeting of the committee of the Council who have the arrangements for the street decorations in hand, was held at the Town Hall yesterday, when they received tenders for the decorations of the streets along the Royal route, and the illuminations of public buildings . . . After considering the designs etc . . . the choice of the committee fell upon Messrs T. Edwards and Sons of High Street, Wolverhampton, who are acting in conjunction with the well-known firm of Messrs. Wormesley of Leeds . . .

There will be at least six triumphal arches on the route . . . with . . . an elaborate specimen at the top of Darlington Street. The arch will be of artistic design, of a rustic character with floral ornamentation, and will also be supplied with electrical illumination. It will consist of eight lofty columns covered with virgin cork, and surmounted by a motto of artistic design, the entire arrangement being intertwined with foliage . . . Palms will be largely employed, and the design generally promises to produce a most pleasing piece of work. This design will, after dusk, be illuminated with a series of vari-coloured 16-candle power electric lamps, ingeniously disposed to produce a pretty and striking artistic effect.

Mayor's Garden Party Abandoned
We are requested to state that owing to the sudden death of Mrs S, S. Mander, the Mayor's mother, the garden party at Wightwick Manor will not take place.

Wednesday July 11 1900
The funeral of Mrs Samuel Small Mander took place today (Wednesday) at 12.30, the remains being interred in the family vault at the cemetery.

. . . The coffin was of polished panelled oak and bore the inscription Mary Mander Born June 7th. 1831 Died July 7th. 1900

July 24, 1900
Wolverhampton was yesterday honoured by a visit on the part of the Duke and Duchess of York, and a thoroughly loyal and enthusiastic welcome was accorded the grandson of her Majesty the Queen, and the Duchess . . . Fortunately the weather was gloriously fine – it was a typical July day, although perhaps a trifle too sultry. From an early hour thousands of people from the surrounding district entered the town and filled the sidewalks of the thoroughfares through which the Royal procession was arranged to pass . . .

The Royal visitors, who are staying for a few days with the Earl and Countess of Dartmouth at their Staffordshire residence, Patsull House, reached Wolverhampton by special train a few minutes after twelve o'clock. The Great Western (Low Level) Railway Station had been most tastefully decorated. Outside . . . there was a blaze of colour, the length of the thoroughfares being canopied with streamers, and inside, the company's staff had covered the bare walls with crimson cloth, and a vast number of flags and banners had been used with charming effect.

. . . their Royal Highnesses were received by the Mayor and Mayoress (Mr and Mrs Theodore Mander) . . . and the Duchess received a bouquet from Miss Marjorie Mander.

The Duchess of York[65] was beautifully dressed in black with sequins, and her toque and parasol matched her gown, being alike trimmed with sequins, while her ornaments were diamonds . . . The Mayoress was wearing a lovely gown of finely-tucked white glacé silk, with transparent yoke and undersleeves, and her white tulle toque was adorned with a bird of paradise plume. At the laying of the foundation stone of the New Free Library, several interesting presentations took place . . . Afterwards the procession wended its way to the Orphanage . . . At the new infirmary of the institution their Royal Highnesses were met by Sir George Chubb, who gave the gold key with which the opening ceremony was performed.

The Duke and Duchess of York at Wightwick 1900.
Back row – Marjorie 6th from the left, Theodore 3rd from the right, the Duke of York 5th from the right.
From row – Flora 4th from the right with the Duchess of York on her right.

. . . Next . . . came the luncheon given by the Mayor to about 400 guests . . . After the luncheon the Royal party proceeded to the large marquee for the distribution of prizes . . . In his reply to the address of thanks, the Duke of York stated the Queen had been graciously pleased to allow the prefix of Royal to be given to the institution which in future would be known as the Royal Orphanage of Wolverhampton. This announcement was greeted with loud acclamations. Then followed the tea provided by Sir Alfred and Lady Hickman.

Interesting Ceremony at Wightwick
After the public ceremonies of Monday an interesting private function took place, we understand, at Wightwick Manor, the residence of the Mayor . . . Before their Royal Highnesses departed for Patsull they planted two trees in the grounds – a purple beech, and a red twigged lime. These had been selected by the Mayor from a number of specimens at Goldthorn Nursery and had been carefully plunged into wooden tubs as long ago as March last by Messrs. Tom B. Dobbs and Co., otherwise they could not have been transplanted at this season of the year.

On the right, The Mayor and the Duchess of York walking up the garden after the tree planting ceremony.

Frankfurt 23/8/1900
Dear Mother,

Thank you very much for the £30 received yesterday . . .

I got back at 10.35 last night after 4 hours in the train from Baden-Baden. Enjoyed the day very much. On Monday went with C.B. and Co. to Heidelberg; and on Tuesday evening with them to the "Fliegende Holländer" (Wagner) I think now of leaving Frankfurt on Sunday 26th . . . getting to Brussels on Sunday night.

Just got your letter of August 22nd. I got the photos alright thanks. Am writing in a tram . . . I will send you a P.C. everyday when I start on my travels, I may have to annex more than the £5 for extra day.

Your L.S. Geoffrey L. Mander.

Newspaper cuttings

Friday September 7 1900
The Mayor of Wolverhampton.
Arrival in Wightwick.
His Worship the Mayor of Wolverhampton (Alderman S. Theodore Mander, B.A.) who has been lying dangerously ill at the Hand Hotel, Llangollen, as a result of contracting an internal chill while out fishing, was removed, under medical advice, to Wightwick on Thursday . . .

Throughout Thursday no one in Wolverhampton received any message from Llangollen, so that the return of the Mayor comes as a surprise. It will be remembered that Alderman Mander went to Llangollen on Saturday week.

The public is anxiously awaiting news that his Worship is out of danger, and fast recovering his wonted strength.

Monday September 10, 1900
The Health of the Mayor.
Operation Performed.
The latest bulletin in regard to the condition of Alderman S. Theodore Mander (Mayor of Wolverhampton) was issued this morning. It says "The Mayor's condition, though still very serious, has considerably improved in the last 24 hours. The Mayor underwent an operation, performed by Dr. Deanesly for internal abscess on Saturday. The operation was born well."

Wednesday September 12 1900
Bulletin
"The Mayor's condition is still grave, but he has had a better night and some of the symptoms have improved."

Saturday, September 15 1900
Death of the Mayor of Wolverhampton
A Useful Career Cut Short.
It is with profound regret that we have to announce the death of Alderman Samuel Theodore Mander, B.A., J.P., Mayor of Wolverhampton, which sad event took place last night at his residence, Wightwick Manor, at half-past nine, after a brief illness contracted at Llangollen. The first news of anything being amiss with Mr Mander was made known to the town twelve days ago . . . when an official announcement was published . . . Inquiries . . . elicited the information that his Worship had been at Llangollen, recruiting after a trying period of official work . . . and had contracted what was described as a chill . . . The symptoms, however, rapidly assumed a gravity which led to Dr. Malet being summoned from Wolverhampton. On Dr. Malet's arrival at Llangollen, he found the Mayor's condition very serious. There were signs of internal inflammation with general blood poisoning . . . so serious did the general symptoms become that . . . Dr. Deanesly was consequently also summoned from Wolverhampton and . . . it was decided that an operation would have to be performed in order to reach the seat of the internal malady. The Mayor himself, we understand, was very anxious to be removed from Llangollen to his own home, and it was decided that the operation should be performed at Wightwick. The Mayor was, therefore, brought home on September 6, the journey being taken under the personal supervision of Dr. Malet, who accompanied the Mayor, the Mayoress also travelling with him . . . A Wolverhampton gentleman, who saw the Mayor as he was being removed to the train at Llangollen, was struck by his appearance, and there was no doubt that his Worship was at that time extremely ill. He bore the railway journey well, being provided with a special carriage . . . On arrival at Wolverhampton, he was placed in an ambulance, and conveyed as carefully as possible to Wightwick Manor, where a fuller and more complete examination

was made . . . As a result, the medical gentlemen discovered the existence of an abscess on the liver, so large that it communicated with the right lung. The doctors, therefore, decided that an operation must be performed for its removal, and Dr. Deanesly, assisted by Dr. Codd, undertook the task . . . But the complications which arose from the general blood condition of the patient showed no improvement . . . On Thursday the Mayor became delirious . . . Yesterday afternoon Mr Percy Dean, surgeon and teacher of operative surgery to the London Hospital met Dr. Deanesly in consultation at Wightwick Manor. It was decided . . . as a last resource to search for a possible deep-seated abscess in the substance of the liver. After a most difficult operation . . . the patient's strength failed suddenly and he succumbed . . . at 9.30 . . . A few people learned the sad news of the death last night, but the majority of the late Mayor's townsmen were made acquainted with the fact this morning by the solemn tolling of St. Peter's minute bell and the presence of flags at half mast over the Town Hall, Higher Grade School, and other public buildings.

The Manse, Shandon, Dumbartonshire. 18th. September 1900
My dear Flora,

I was very grieved indeed to read the announcement of your husband's death in the Glasgow paper yesterday and write at once to offer you my warmest sympathy in your sudden bereavement . . . I Know only Our Father and time can heal the wound and nothing any earthly friend can say will do much good . . . I do pray that Jesus may comfort both you and the children . . . I know you will not care to write for some time, but when you can I will be glad to hear from you. I always have such happy memories of the times I spent with you at Wolverhampton and of your and Mr Mander's kindness.

With love and deepest sympathy dear Flora,
Yours affectionately, Annie S. Miller.[66]

The Horniman Museum, Forest Hill, London. S.E. September 18th. 1900
Dear Mrs Mander,

I have only just seen the announcement of the sad death of your dear husband. I am truly grieved and beg to offer you my sincere sympathy in your great trial.

He was my Chairman for the three years while I was Curator at the Art Gallery, and when I left he gave me an excellent testimonial which I shall ever prize and which I believe had great weight in obtaining for me my present appointment as Curator to the above.

With kind regards, I remain, Yours sincerely, Richard Quick.

The Morritt Arms, Greta Bridge. Barnard Castle. September 22
Dear Mrs Mander,

I was shocked and grieved to see a few days ago in a Scotch paper a notice of Mr Mander's death, and though I had seen him so little I feel that I must write and tell you how deeply I sympathize with you in your great sorrow. It seems very hard that he should be taken away in the middle of a life of so much activity and usefulness.

Please accept my sincere sympathy and believe me, yours truly,
Alfred Parsons.

An account of Theodore Mander's Civic Funeral follows, taken from several newspapers

Tuesday September 18th 1900

The day was well in keeping with the occasion, for though the sun at times shone out with brightness, there was an ominous moaning of the wind, such as one notices as the prelude of a coming storm . . .

At Wightwick
So many of the places of business had been closed because of the event, so many schools were silent, so subdued were all by the solemnity of the day that it seemed like a calm Sabbath morn . . . the general public had refrained from going to Wightwick, and the only spectators were one or two cyclists brought from afar and the little groups of sympathetic villagers, no one intruding upon the privacy of the bereaved family.

At ten minutes to eleven the coffin containing the remains of the deceased was carried through the main entrance by a number of the estate servants and placed on the open hearse . . . On the coffin were placed the deceased's cocked hat and dress sword betokening his office . . . The four splendid horses drew the hearse forward, and the mourning party rapidly took their places in the carriages. The order of the coaches was as follows:-

First carriage – Rev. R.F. Horton[67], Rev. C. Dunkley, Dr. Deanesly
Hearse
Second carriage – Mrs S.T. Mander, Miss Marjorie Mander
Third carriage – Mr Geoffrey Mander, Mr Lionel Mander,
Mr Alan Mander
Fourth carriage – Mr Charles Mander, Mr C.A. Mander, Mr B.H. Mander
Fifth carriage – Mr H. Clarke, Mr Neville H. Mander
Sixth Carriage – Dr. R. Felkin, Dr. Fraser, Mr R. Pearsall
Seventh carriage – Mr M.J. Smythe, Mr C.J. Smythe, Professor Hannay

Eighth carriage – Mr A.J. Soames, Mr F.C. Davis-Colley

The procession started at 11 o'clock down the steep lane to the Bridgnorth Road, up which the late Mayor had been carried for the last time a few days before. The Mermaid Inn looked for once uninviting with all its blinds drawn and its door severely closed. All down the road to Compton little groups of bareheaded spectators sorrowfully watched the passing of their dead friend and all the blinds of the houses en route were drawn. At Compton it was the same, the whole of the inhabitants seeming to be out on the footpaths.

As the sad procession neared Chapel Ash, the detached groups became a continuous stream, while the flags on all buildings were at half-mast, and the places of business were all closed. Some of the patients at the Eye Infirmary were noticeable in the grounds of that institution, while the building was also in mourning. On Compton Road the melancholy sound of "the passing bell" tolling in the steeple of St. Mark's was heard, and the crowd became of considerable proportions. The churchyard was filled with spectators and all the neighbouring coigns of vantage were also occupied.

In Darlington Street the scene was most impressive, the footpaths being lined with a silent crowd. The workmen on the new Wesleyan Church had stopped work in sympathy, and were gathered on the scaffolding to watch the cortege pass. Queen Square was packed with further mourners, and from thence to Queen Street Church the procession passed through a vast orderly throng, whose sympathetic bearing was most marked.

At The Town Hall

The procession consisting of members of the Wolverhampton Town Council, School Board, Board of Guardians, officials, and those of other public bodies in the borough, was formed in the vestibule of the Town Hall, and left that building in the following order at eleven o'clock:-

Chief Constable (Captain Burnett), the Mayor's Sergeant, carrying the mace and chain draped in crape, and the Mayor's robes; the Town Clerk in wig and gown; and Aldermen . . . Councillors . . . Public Officials . . . Members of Parliament . . . Magistrates . . . Board of Guardians . . . School Board . . . Volunteers . . . Yeomanry . . . Chamber of Commerce . . . Law Society . . . Staffordshire County Council . . . Ministers of Religion . . . Wolverhampton Royal Orphanage . . . South Wolverhampton Liberal Association . . . It was with no little trouble that those responsible for the procession from the Town Hall to the Queen Street Chapel managed to restore order within the vestibule so numerous were the representatives of the various societies and bodies who had come to pay their last tribute of respect to the dead Mayor . . . the procession started to the tolling of St. Peter's bell. The route was lined with the usual concourse of sightseers, who were wedged into congested masses at those points where more than a passing glimpse of the proceedings could be obtained.

To the church where his form was so familiar – where members of the Mander family have for years worshipped – the body of Wolverhampton's Mayor was borne. Long before the time appointed the precincts of the famous edifice, around which so many memories dear to Nonconformists cluster, were thronged by townspeople. At half-past ten the doors were thrown open, and the worshippers filed in . . . With silent respectful tread and bowed heads, the people took up the seats allotted to them. By previous arrangement the employees of the deceased gentleman occupied the seats under the galleries downstairs and the two front [rows of] seats in the great gallery. The members of the Corporation filled the front seats in the centre, the chief mourners being seated on the opposite side . . .

Just before eleven o'clock the deceased's employees entered the church, and a few minutes sufficed to find them seated . . . The dark raiment of those assembled contrasted strongly with the summer-like profusion of foliage in the vicinity of the pulpit . . . and choir gallery. The pulpit was adorned with asparagus fern . . . amongst a glory of palms, caladiums and ferns, with here and there a delicate white or red flower. From the organ gallery were suspended baskets of ferns . . .

The first note of the organ, at which Mr Amos Keay presided, broke the solemn, painful silence . . . Soon afterwards the beautiful, confident strains of "I know that my Redeemer liveth," uprose, the familiar notes having a sad appropriateness on this occasion, recalling the faith to which the late Mayor at all times held fast . . .

At twenty minutes past eleven came the echo of footsteps in the vestibule . . . The vast assembly rose and then the procession entered. The mace-bearer led the way, but the . . . glitter of the civic badge was obscured by the draperies of death . . . While the members of the Corporation, and those who walked with them were taking their seats, the congregation remained standing. All eyes were turned in the direction of the Mayoral robes and chain . . . which were placed . . . in front of the Communion table. A few minutes later the deacons of Queen Street Church entered . . . This had scarcely taken place ere the coffin was wheeled into the church. Tearful eyes watched its progress . . . and noted the beautiful wreath, the Court sword, and the cocked hat.

At this moment Dr. Horton ascended the pulpit, followed by the present pastor (Mr F. Lenwood B.A.) The two stood with heads bowed in prayer, the entire congregation on its feet. Then Mr Lenwood's sympathetic voice was heard announcing the hymn . . . The subsequent passages of Scripture . . . were read by Mr Lenwood, and then it was that Dr. R.F. Horton rose to speak. His voice trembled perceptibly. When a man who has filled a public station . . . is called away by death, it was, he reminded the congregation, legitimate and becoming that we should give expression to some thoughts and feelings which under other circumstances are kept locked up in the silence of our breasts . . .

Then Dr. Horton spoke of his life-long friendship with the deceased, and the days "when we were boys together" at school and elsewhere . . . "I shall try" said he "in a few words to lay, as it were, a tribute upon the coffin of my friend, and of your fellow citizen." Then he spoke of the honoured name of Mander, which name the deceased had left now doubly honoured. The late Mayor's entry into the public life of the town was alluded to . . . Dr. Horton next spoke of the deceased's deep religious nature . . . The congregation then had a telling picture of the man true to conviction, who never lets the spirit of bigotry enter his thought or warp his action . . . Closing an impressive address, Dr. Horton said "we are thankful to know that he leaves behind him those who bear his name, and we fervently pray that they will bear his spirit, and his principles, and his devotion too . . ."

The preacher's voice was lifted in prayer for a few minutes, and then the hymn with the closing lines:-

"Father in Thy gracious keeping,
Leave we now Thy servant sleeping"

was sung. The congregation yet waited for the seal to the funeral service – the soul-thrilling noble strains of the "Dead March" in Saul.

When the organ ceased its peal the coffin was removed, and a start made for its final resting place.

. . . It was one o'clock before the funeral procession was re-formed, and started on the last journey to Pattingham[68] . . . The procession had been greatly increased by the addition of a large number of private carriages, and its progress was in consequence, considerably slower than before. The weather had taken a turn for the worse, and . . . spots of rain were felt heralding a sharp downfall, while the bells of the Collegiate Church rang out a funeral peal, which seemed more than ever appropriate.

The procession was on this occasion headed by the members of the Corporation, the School Board, public officials, deputations etc. who marched as far as Compton Road, and then formed a guard of honour, through which the cortege passed. The sight of these long rows of leading citizens, standing silently in the pitiful rain in their official costumes, formed a fitting adieu from Wolverhampton to its late head.

. . . Pattingham was reached at 2.30. All blinds were drawn in neighbourly sympathy, and the inhabitants stood at their doors, while the bell of the church was rung . . . Fourteen of the deceased's employees met the coffin at the gate and carried it to the grave. This was to the right of the pathway beneath a fine tree. It was lined with moss, and the edge was strewn with ivy and choice flowers. The Rev. Dr. Horton read the brief service, and the Rev. C. Dunkley . . . offered up the benedictory prayer. The last words spoken, all took a parting glance at the coffin as it lay in its last resting place, and then Samuel Theodore Mander was left – an honoured name.

From Flora's wreath.

"Revered, beloved, who camest to thy goal
So early, leaving me behind,
I would the great world grew like thee,
Who grewest not alone in power,
In knowledge, but by years and hours
In reverence and in charity."

ENDNOTES

1. Ref. humanitarianism

   Extracts from a Minute book of the Mander firm. H.C. was Henry Clark, the London and Foreign manager of the firm 1868 – 1901.

   "At a Meeting held at the Offices on Monday, November 27th 1865. Present – The Firm and H.C.

   . . . H.C. proposed that it might be advisable to pay a Medical man a fixed stipend to furnish attendance and medicine to all the workpeople and that his certificate should be required when anyone may be absent through ill health."

   Extract from meeting held on Thursday January 22nd. 1866.

   . . . "It was agreed that all persons on the works should be provided with Medical attendance gratis."

   Nearly 70 years later, in 1932, the firm was the first in the country to establish a 40 hour week in a number of its departments.

2. Theodore was seven months old when Samuel Mander took the fashionable "Malvern Cure." There are no direct references anywhere else to his illness, but he may have had arthritis; later in his life it is obvious that writing became difficult. The austere water cure establishment was run by Doctor Gully, together with Doctors Wilson and Grindrod; it was said that the purity of the water produced the cures.

3. Basford House, Whalley Range, Manchester was the home of Samuel Mander's sister Jemima who married H.B. Jackson in 1829.

4. Henry Day is mentioned in Theodore's holiday diary written during his 1878 visit to America.

He travelled to England regularly and after Theodore's marriage stayed at Wightwick. His first entry in the visitors' book is dated May 1891 "Henry Day came in May and went away, that is all he has to say. This is original." After another visit in May 1896 he wrote "seven days, all brilliant red letter days."

5. From "A Tettenhall History" and "History of Tettenhall College" both by Geoffrey Hancock.

The school was opened in 1863 ". . . with fifteen boys and a cow. The latter was no doubt to provide the boys with milk and some of the earliest accounts of the College relate to this animal. "'Paid for lotions for the cow – 1/6d' or 'paid for a milking stool and a hundred weight of coal – 1/2d.'"

The interest shown by Samuel Mander in physical training for the young may have influenced the other proprietors of the school. A gymnasium was built between 1863 and 1864 and a swimming pool in 1876 – both fairly unusual in schools of this period.

As early as 1870 it was agreed that the school should be known as Tettenhall College.

In 1916 the shareholders system was abolished and a Trust established to be managed by a Board of Governors ensuring, for the first time, that all profits would be invested in the school.

In 1929 a former pupil of the school, Dr. Arthur Harden, was awarded the Nobel prize for Chemistry.

6. ". . . the Cambridge examination" was the principal external examination at Tettenhall College. Theodore took the Junior section in 1866 and the Senior exam in 1870.

Robert Horton *see* endnote 63.

Cousin Mander was Mander Smyth, the son of Samuel Mander's sister, Elizabeth. At one time he was a traveller for the family firm in the Birmingham district. He became manager of the Colour (paints) department and remained there until 1905.

7. Baedeker (1894) refers to the decorative head-dresses worn by many women in the places visited by Theodore and his father.

"The inhabitants are more primitive in their habits than those of Southern Holland, and adhere more tenaciously to the picturesque costumes of their ancestors. The head-dress of the women is often curious. It consists of a broad band of gold . . . decorated at the sides with large oval rosettes of the same metal . . . The inhabitants of Friesland, who are often met with in Amsterdam . . . wear a kind of skull cap of metal, usually silver gilt . . . finished with spiral ornaments." Theodore thought that the metal decorations were brass ". . . These trinkets are generally of gold, even among the poorer classes, or at least of silver, and are handed down from mother to daughter as heir-looms"

8. Theodore's statement in his letter of March 11th 1868 "the cellars at Glen Bank are being roofed over" suggests that the house was built by Samuel Mander in 1868. It stood in extensive grounds next to the Towers, a large house later acquired by its other neighbour, Tettenhall Proprietary School.

   After Samuel Mander died, his widow Mary continued to live at Glen Bank until her death in 1900. The house and land was sold to John Marston (founder of the Sunbeam Motor Car Company.) His daughter Ida married Edward Deanesly, the surgeon who attended Theodore during his final illness.

   In the 1970's the house was demolished. The Wolverhampton Nuffield Hospital was opened on the site in 1978.

9. Robert Felkin was Manager of the Home Department at Mander Bros. and also Company Secretary.

10. Theodore was most probably referring to John Shaw (Shawe) 1608 – 1672 the puritan preacher, whose autobiography "Memoirs of the Life of John Shawe" was published in 1824. His determination to preach and to propagate his beliefs despite constant difficulties, obviously appealed to Theodore, particularly as the D.N.B. states "It appears he was a Congregationalist in his ideas of church government . . ."

11. John Fraser M.D., F.G.S., F.R.C.S. Edin. 1820 – 1909. On a plaque outside his house at No. 5 Tettenhall Road, Wolverhampton, he is described as – "Botanist and Geologist" together with the information that – "Wolverhampton Art Gallery and Museum houses his collection of 10,000 fossils and minerals."

12. John Huss/Jan Hus c. 1369-1415 – was a religious reformer from Bohemia. Influenced by the teaching of Wyclif, he denounced ecclesiastical abuses and challenged the authority of Rome. In 1410 he was excommunicated. He accepted the safe conduct offered by Sigismund which enabled him to attend the Council of Constance held in 1414 However, at Constance he was condemned and burnt at the stake as a heretic.

   Jerome of Prague c 1370-1416 attempted to defend Huss at the Council of Constance and he too was denounced as a heretic and executed.

13. Chalybeate water is impregnated with iron salts.

14. When Theodore arrived in Paris at the end of July 1871 it was only 2 months after the end of the Franco-Prussian War.

Paris had been under siege from September 1870 until the city capitulated in January 1871. It was during this siege that a Parisian butcher bought the animals from the Zoo and sold their meat. Elephant's trunk meat was sold eventually for 50 francs per pound.

Shortly after the siege was lifted, the Paris Commune was proclaimed by workers and intellectuals in opposition to the French government. The most famous act of rebellion took place in the Place Vendome when the column, topped by a statue of Napoleon, was felled.

The Commune was eventually suppressed, in May 1871, after the government troops and the Communards fought pitched battles in the streets of Paris.

It was the evidence of these battles that Theodore reported in his notebook.

In the records of Mander Brothers it was noted that in 1871 the firm's stock "had a simply miraculous escape, having been discovered by the leaders of the commune only a few hours before the final events of that bloody strife."

Messrs Levy and Feinger were the French agents for Mander Brothers in France. From 1865 they also managed the Belgian agency.

Eventually a Levy daughter married into the Feinger family; they visited Wightwick in 1889 and signed the visitors' book "Levy-Feinger."

15. Ref. William Mortimer – from "A Tettenhall History" by Geoffrey Hancock

" . . . they marched in crocodile . . . each Sunday down to Queen Street Chapel, escorted by the School Sargeant, an impressively clad figure, who had served in India during the Mutiny and had saved his life, so he told the boys, by swimming over a mile down the Ganges."

16. Ref. "The Higher Criticism" – this was the title given to the rigorous debates on the intellectual and aesthetic content of the Bible. See Thomas Hardy's poem "The Respectable Burgher on 'The Higher Criticism'" – Thomas Hardy, Selected Poems. Penguin (Page 247)

17. The ill-fated expedition referred to by Theodore set out from Lauber's Inn on July 13th. 1865. The party of 7 was the first to reach the summit of the Matterhorn but during the descent a rope broke and all but three members of the group were killed. Later, Lauber's Inn was renamed the Monte Rosa Hotel.

18. Ref. to the Rev. Gregory belonging to "the lowest of the Low . . ." This is a reference to Low church membership.

19. The Rev. Roger's sermon was based on the quotation from the First Epistle of John – "And the world passeth away, and the lust thereof: but he that doeth the will of God abideth for ever."

20. Ref. "Love in the Time of Victoria" by Francoise Barret-Ducrocq. Penguin

The Foundling Hospital – opened on March 25th. 1741 by Thomas Coram.

It was originally simply a refuge for unwanted children, but soon after its establishment it was felt that such an institution could encourage prostitution and the admissions committee eventually changed certain policies. Only illegitimate children under one year were admitted; they could be accepted for a limited period or permanently.

Theodore's belief that the children had been rescued from "abodes of filth and misery" was not completely accurate. From the records of the Foundling Hospital it is apparent that many mothers tried but were unable to earn enough money to support their children, and were forced to place them in the Foundling Hospital with the greatest reluctance. The pathetic tokens listed by Theodore "brooches, necklaces, coins, nails, pins, wire etc." left as a means of identification show clearly that the wall text "When my father and mother forsake me . . ." could not be applied to all the children.

Many mothers hoped that their children would stay only for a short time; occasionally mothers married and were able to reclaim their children.

21. The Rev, Stopford Brooke was the great-grandfather of Peter Brooke (Secretary of State for National Heritage 1993.) He was an early member of the Society for the Protection of Ancient Buildings: at the first meeting held on March 27 1887, William Morris was appointed Honorary Secretary.

22. Flora Elvira St. Clair Paint was 17 when she visited the Mander family for the first time: her grandparents came from Guernsey (ref. parish register of St. Pierre du Bois.) On her marriage certificate the profession of her father, Henry Paint, is "merchant," – later he became an M.P. in the Canadian Parliament.

23. Ellen Pearsall was Theodore's cousin.

24. August Wilhelm Hofmann (1818-1892) was at one time superintendent at the Royal College of Chemistry in London. Later, in Berlin, he was noted for his experiments on coal tar. In 1863 he produced a basic dye known as Hofmann's Violet.

25. ". . . some wash" refers to taking in washing to earn money.

26. Antoine Wiertz (1806-1865) – a Belgian artist whose government built him a studio in Brussels in 1850, now the Wiertz Museum.

27. "Miss Beyerhaus' establishment" was a school at No. 3 Hainer Weg, run by Miss Maria Beyerhaus.

28. Friedrich August Kekule von Stradonitz (1829-1896) German chemist who discovered the ring structure of benzene and other organic compounds.

Robert Wilhelm Bunsen (1811-1899) German chemist whose name will always be associated with the development of the Bunsen burner. He was 63 when Theodore described him as "very old."

Robert William Felkin was the son of Robert Felkin – see endnote 9. He was studying in Chemnitz; his uncle Henry Felkin lived at Karlmarxstadt. Robert William married Mary (Polly) in 1882. There is a letter in the Wightwick archives from their son Samuel Denys Felkin, in which he states "Samuel not Small after Grandfather." Following the family tradition he was always known as Denys.

29. Mr Davies – the Berlin agent for the British and Foreign Bible Society.

30. The advantage of working in the Inorganic laboratory meant that with the absence of English speaking students his German should improve.

31. John Street – initially 48 John Street, Wolverhampton was the home of the Manders and the place where their first varnish works was established. To one side of the garden were the buildings used by Benjamin Mander (1752-1819) in his business as japanner and tin-plate worker. The chemical and drug works owned by his brother John (1754-1827) stood next door.

According to family tradition Benjamin's son Charles began experimenting with the production of varnishes in the John Street house but he was soon banished to a shed at the bottom of the garden after a small explosion in the kitchen. Eventually the site was taken over completely by the varnish works and expanded further in 1890 when the adjoining John Street Chapel was added to the factory.

32. The earliest official registry of an exchange rate between Berlin and England was 1893 with her little change during the previous 50 years.
36 groschen = 1 thaler
1 thaler = 3 German marks
20.40 German markes = £1 English.

33. Alexander Murdoch Mackay (1849-1890) – He studied engineering at Edinburgh University. When Theodore met him, he had been working in Berlin for nearly a year and studying the language. The "machine manufactory" eventually promoted him to the position of chief of the locomotive department. He lived in Berlin with the family of Pastor Baur see page 99. His first attempt in 1875 to become a missionary was unsuccessful, however a year later he was accepted by the Church Missionary Society and he arrived in Zanzibar in May 1876; because of sickness and constant instability and bloodshed within the country it took over two years before he reached Uganda where he lived for 14 years. From 1884 he had increased suspicion and hostility to combat but always hoped to establish a permanent Christian station in Uganda. He died of malaria in February 1890, the last member of his 1876 missionary group.

34. It is possible that this letter was written by Nellie for Samuel Mander during an attack of arthritis.

35. Theodore was concluding the short period of practical work in Vienna referred to in his father's letter of February the 22nd 1875.

36. Lord Dufferin was the Governor-General of Canada 1872 – 1878
He was followed by the Marquess of Lorne 1878 – 1883.

37. The exchange rates between Canada and England did not alter between 1875 and 1880. In 1878/79 Canadian/English business was conducted in "Canadian Sterling' which translated into English currency as £9 Canadian = £10 English sterling.

The earliest exchange rate for Canadian dollars was established in 1895 when £1 English sterling = 4.80 Canadian dollars.

38. Arthur Tippet was Theodore's second cousin. See reference 39 below.

39. H. Grendon Tippet married Theodore's cousin Edith Harriet Jackson of Basford House, Whalley Range, Manchester; Arthur was their second son.

40. In 1878/79 there were separate exchange rates for all U.S. states with an average variation of 1%

In New York State in 1878 £1 English sterling = 4.823 U.S. dollars

1879 £1 English sterling = 4.839 U.S. dollars

41. Mary P: this is Mary le Mesurier Paint, Flora's sister. She was born in 1859, and so at the time of the visit of Theodore and Mima would have been about 19. She married Theodore's cousin Charles Tertius Mander in 1884. They lived at the Mount, a house standing in grounds close to Wightwick Manor and redesigned in part by Edward Ould, the architect of Wightwick. Both houses were about a mile from Glen Bank. Charles Mander was created a baronet in 1911 and died in 1929. Mary died in 1951 aged 92.

The Mount was sold after her death and is now an hotel.

42. Philip Vale joined Mander Bros. in 1863. He was among the works staff celebrating the 21st. birthday of Theodore's cousin Charles at the Mount in 1873 and he added to the general hilarity during the party by falling into a pond.

43. Flora and Theodore's first child, Gladys, died shortly after her birth.

44. The Dampkjokken (steam kitchen) was a large establishment for the benefit of the poor. Meals could be eaten on the premises at big marble topped tables and customers could also take their food away.

In 1883 a krone = 1s. 1d (approximately) and an ore = 1/100 of a krone.

45. Strom-parterren was a restaurant on Stromsborg a small island, where there were also baths and where music was played during the afternoon and evening.

Hasselbacken was the largest and best of the numerous cafes and restaurants in the area.

46. The province of Dalecarlia – according to Baedeker (1882) "The inhabitants of the banks of Lake Siljan . . . have preserved many of their primitive characteristics. They are generally poor . . . In their ideas of cleanliness they are somewhat behind the age . . . The best time to visit Lake Siljan is in the height of summer, when the vegetation is in perfection, and when the younger members of the community while away the long twilight with dances around the richly decked village may-poles."

A small wooden painted horse, from Dalecarlia, stands on the mantelpiece in the day nursery at Wightwick.

47. The first electric street lighting in Britain was installed on Holborn Viaduct in London in 1878.

48. Oscar Wilde was well known for the way in which he appropriated ideas and used them in his lectures; many of William Morris' pronouncements appear presented as original thought, one being the statement noted by Theodore beginning "Do not use anything which you do not know to be useful . . ." A famous anecdote, illustrating his friends' awareness of this tendency, describes how, after overhearing a witty remark, Wilde sighed "I wish I'd said that" to which a friend replied "You will Oscar! You will!"

49. Professor Tyndall (1820-1893) He lectured at the Royal Institution where, in 1853, he succeeded Faraday as superintendent; he followed him also as scientific advisor to Trinity House and the Board of Trade. He was a friend of Thomas Huxley with whom he undertook a number of geological investigations. They produced "The Glaciers of the Alps" in 1860.

50. Mr Hoare probably worked in his family's business at Hoare's Bank in Fleet Street. It was founded at the end of the 17th century by Sir Richard Hoare who became Lord Mayor of London in 1712. His son Henry built Stourhead, famous for its gardens and now owned by the National Trust.

51. The inscription on the first page of the visitors' book is "Names of guests who have spent one or more nights at Mornington Place, Wolverhampton. November 1879" then added later "and at Wightwick Manor 1889."

Many of Theodore and Flora's visitors were members of the family, but also there were friends who were mentioned in Theodore's journals, for example, Arthur Bayfield with whom Theodore and his cousin Mander Smyth visited Normandy.

Some of the people Theodore met in the course of his public duties visited Wightwick. In 1894 staying at the same time as Charles Dunkley, St Mary's Vicarage – see the account of the civic funeral – was William Macdonald Sinclair, Archdeacon of London. St Paul's E.C.

Another entry reads:- Isobel Somerset, Eastnor Castle May 14th, 1900.

Lady Henry Somerset was in Wolverhampton at that time to attend a meeting of the Midland Temperence League.

52. Since Theodore's visit, Spearpoint has been extended and is now an hotel – The Master Spearpoint, Canterbury Road, Ashford.

53. There is a noticeable gap in the archive papers relating to the period between 1887 and 1893 when Theodore Mander was involved in planning,

building and extending Wightwick Manor. There are none of the letters one might expect to find from Edward Ould, with suggestions and inquiries about the design of the new house. The bills for the 1887 wing were found only in the 1980's; they were sandwiched between the inner and outer doors of the serving hatch of the 1887 dining room (now the library) but attempts to find more papers relating to this period have been unsuccessful. The records of Grayson and Ould were destroyed in an air raid during the last war.

An issue of "The Architect" produced between 1887 and 1893, before Wightwick was extended, featured an article on the Turkish bath which had been installed in the house:-

"The plan and description of Mr. S.T. Mander's private Turkish bath at Wightwick Manor, Wolverhampton, Messrs. Grayson and Ould, architects, Liverpool, will be of interest to many of our readers. The building which is of brick, consists of three rooms – two hot rooms and a cooling room . . . The inside walls are of glazed bricks in various colours, designed in good taste. These walls form the best surface for hot-rooms; they are easily washed . . . The bath is effectively heated by Messrs. J. Constantine and Son's (Manchester) Convoluted Stove. The size of warm-air flue is 2 feet 9 inches. The air to be heated is drawn from outside through flues of equal dimensions. With such provision for ventilation a rapid and constant change of air takes place and all vitiated air and the effluva thrown off by the bather is speedily carried away, and one of the chief desiderata of bathers secured much to their satisfaction . . ."

When Wightwick was extended in 1893, the cooling room was removed and the area incorporated into the new back corridor leading from the kitchen to the new dining room. The two remaining rooms have been restored and are on view to the public. It seems that this Turkish bath and the one at Cragside in Northumberland (N.T.) are the only 19th century Turkish baths installed in private houses which have survived.

54. Ref " . . . the lane opposite Uncle H" Uncle Harper lived at Wightwick House next door to Wightwick Manor. It is possible that Theodore and Flora stayed with him when plans for Wightwick were being drawn up. The visitors' book for 1886 has "Wightwick House" beside the date.

55. Richardson of Darlington – Founded in 1874, the firm built glasshouses and conservatories. As the factory stood next to the railway line with its own siding, it sent out all the materials by rail with a separate carriage attached to the rear of the train to carry the construction workers. The firm designed and installed heating systems as well – those in the cathedrals of Lincoln

and York were supplied by Richardsons. After 100 years the firm ran into difficulties but was saved by a merger with another Darlington firm, Amdega.

The glass house at Wightwick was restored to working condition in 1994. Many of the original features have survived.

56. Ref. the Countess of Dartmouth. The 6th Earl of Dartmouth and his wife lived about 6 miles from Wightwick at Patsull Hall.

William Legge, the 4th Earl of Dartmouth bought Patsull Hall in 1848.

He lived at Sandwell Hall on the outskirts of West Bromwich and it is thought that he acquired Patsull in order to provide his son, Viscount Lewisham, with a base for his activities as M.P. for South Staffordshire. The 6th. Earl succeeded to the title in 1891. The family lived at Patsull until 1963.

57. One of the first teachers at Wightwick Manor School was Miss A. Drew. She returned to Wolverhampton years later as the wife of the headmaster of the Grammar School, Mr Watson Caldicott. One of the pupils at Wightwick was Gerald Poynton Mander (1885-1951) the younger son of Charles and Mary Mander (Flora's sister) He became a governor of the Grammar School in 1914 and then chairman of the governors from 1934 until his death.

58. Apley Park, Shropshire is a Gothick house built in 1811 for Thomas Whitmore on a site formerly occupied in succession by at least 3 other houses.

Davenport House, Shropshire stands on the edge of the village of Worfield, between Wolverhampton and Bridgnorth. It was built in 1726 for Henry Davenport, by Francis Smith of Warwick. The present heir William Davenport, will inherit the house when he is 24. Before his father died in 1990 he arranged for Davenport House to be rented for 20 years by a restaurant business and for most of its contents to be loaned to the National Trust.

59. "Trysull with B.H.M . . ." Trysull Manor, about 3 miles from Wightwick, was the home of Theodore's brother Howard.

60. Netherton was the head gardener's house but it is now privately owned; its small ponds still can be glimpsed through the hedges beside the pools at Wightwick Manor.

61. Alfred Parsons (1847-1920) As well as working as a garden designer he was

a painter and one of his landscapes hangs in the Acanthus Room at Wightwick.

62. The Mermaid Inn was built to serve the passing trade from the nearby canal; oblique references to the public house can be found in some of the external carving at Wightwick where several mermaids coil round the walls, together with dogs, owls and flowers.

63. The account of Queen Victoria's brief visit to Wolverhampton was compiled using cuttings from two local papers and from The Daily News, The Daily Express and The Times.

    There are several large books full of newspaper cuttings from local and national papers in the archives at Wightwick, and all the reports used in the text are from this source.

64. Emma Smith became housekeeper at Wightwick. While Flora was living in Switzerland and Rome, from October 1900 Emma Smith wrote a series of interesting letters to her full of all the news from Wightwick.

65. The Duchess of York was in mourning for her father, the Duke of Teck.

    George V (the Duke of York) came to the throne in 1910. Queen Mary (the Duchess of York) lived to see her grand-daughter, Elizabeth 11, succeed to the throne in 1952.

66. Annie Miller née Sempleton – see the letter of November 7th 1877.

67. Dr. Robert Horton was one of the first pupils at Tettenhall Proprietary School and one of its most brilliant scholars. He won an Open Scholarship to Oxford where he gained a Double First; he was the first Non-Conformist to become President of the Union. In 1879, his was the first signature in Theodore and Flora's visitors' book.

68. Pattingham is a village half way between Wightwick and Patsull.

For more than two years after Theodore's death Flora travelled in Europe, never settling anywhere for long. In October, a month after her husband's funeral she went to live in Switzerland, and for two months in 1901 she stayed in Rome. In April 1901 she returned to London and from there travelled to Wightwick but at the end of June she was back in London.

At last, in September 1903, Flora returned to Wightwick and after a gap of three years there were entries in the visitors' book again.

In April 1905, she died, like Theodore, aged 47 at a nursing home in Welbeck Street in London.

With the exception of Mima, all Theodore's brothers and sisters married. Howard became a director of Mander Brothers: Martin emigrated to New Zealand and became a sheep farmer.

At the time of his father's death Geoffrey Mander was at Trinity College, Cambridge, where he studied organic chemistry. In 1906 he married a Canadian, Rosalind Caverhill; they had three children. They were divorced in 1930 and shortly after this he married Rosalie Glynn Grylls by whom he had a son and daughter. Like his father, Geoffrey Mander was a Liberal member of Wolverhampton Council and in 1929 he was elected as Liberal M.P. for East Wolverhampton. He eventually lost his seat in the 1945 election, the year in which he was knighted.

After an unsuccessful attempt to sell Wightwick in 1920, the house was accepted by the National Trust in December 1937.

Sir Geoffrey Mander died at Wightwick in 1962 aged 80.

Some time after the death of her mother, Marjorie decided to join her Uncle Martin and his wife Stella in New Zealand and help to look after their children. It was there that she met Gervas Nevile.

He was born at Skellingthorpe Manor, near Lincoln and educated at Winchester and Cambridge. After a brief, unsuccessful career as a stock-broker he attended Cirencester Agricultural College. While he was at Cambridge he met Arthur Mander (eldest son of Charles and Mary Mander and 2nd. baronet) and visited The Mount; eventually he was put in touch with Martin Mander who employed him on the farm in New Zealand.

On the 1910 marriage certificate of Marjorie and Gervas Nevile "in the district of Gisborne, New Zealand" their professions are entered as "Shepherd" and "Domestic duties." By the time their son was born in 1912 they had moved to Auckland and he was a sheep farmer.

Marjorie Mander died in 1953.

In a letter of sympathy sent to Geoffrey Mander on his mother's death, Lionel (just 17) and Alan (14) were described as "difficult," perhaps something to be expected after five very disturbed years.

In February 1912 Lionel married Princess Pretiva, the sister of the Maharajah of Cooch Behar. They were divorced in the 1920's and Lionel married Kathleen French by whom he had a son.

After the First War, in which he served in the Royal Flying Corps, Lionel became an actor, writer and film director; he acted in "The Pleasure Garden" an early Hitchcock film made in 1926. Two of his plays were produced in London in 1927 and 1930. He moved then to Hollywood where he appeared in over 60 films under the name Miles Mander and where he became well known as a reliable character actor. He played Cardinal Richelieu in "The Three Musketeers," starring Basil Rathbone and he appeared as Ginger Rogers' father in "The Primrose Path." In the 1939 production by William Wyler of "Wuthering Heights" starring Laurence Olivier and Merle Oberon, he played Mr Lockwood.

In 1946 Lionel Mander died in Hollywood aged 57.

After his mother's death, while he was quite young, Alan was sent to sea where he spent two unhappy years aboard the last of the old tea clippers, the "Port Jackson," sailing between London and Sydney.

In 1913 he accompanied Lionel's wife on a visit to her sister, Princess Sudhira, who was ill in a London nursing home. A tempestuous courtship began, which was opposed by her family, but eventually Alan and Princess Sudhira were married in 1914 in Calcutta. They had two daughters and a son.

Alan was always very proud of his Scottish ancestry which Flora's children could trace through their grandmother's family, the MacVeans of Colonsay, Co. Argyle – from a very early age, there are many photographs of him wearing the kilt. It was because of his Scottish connections that in the First War, Alan was able to join the King's Own Cameron Highlanders; he served for two years in the trenches before being invalided out with shell-shock. During this time his wife was a V.A.D. at Westminster Hospital. Alan also served in the Second War as a Squadron Leader in the R.A.F.

He died in December 1968; his wife Sudhira suffered a stroke and died 17 days later.

BENJAMIN MANDER *b.* 1752 *d.* 1819
m.
ELIZABETH HANBURY READ

CHARLES MANDER *b.* 1780 *d.* 1853
m.
JEMIMA SMALL *b.* 1791 *d.* 1834

- Elizabeth *b.* 1815 *m.* J.F. Smyth
  - Mander Smyth
- Jemima *b.* 1817 *m.* H.B. Jackson
  - Gertrude
  - Edith
  - 5 others
- Charles *b.* 1819 *m.* Sophia Weaver
  - Charles Tertius Ist baronet *b.* 1852 *m.* Mary Paint *b.* 1859
- SAMUEL SMALL *b.* 1822 *m.* MARY WILKES
  - S.THEODORE *b.* 1853 *m.* FLORA PAINT *b.* 1857
    - Geoffrey *b.* 1882
    - Marjorie *b.* 1883
    - Lionel *b.* 1888
    - Alan *b.* 1891
  - Mary *b.* 1853 *m.* Robert Felkin
  - Mima *b.* 1857
  - Nellie *b.* 1858 *m.* Howard Pearsall
  - Lotte *b.* 1860 *m.* ...Parker
  - Howard *b.* 1861 *m.* Lilian ...
  - Martin *b.* 1869 *m.* Stella ...
- Janetta *b.* 1823 *m.* Henry Harper